YOUR GUIDE TO BETTER TRAINING

DISCOVER THE SECRETS TO BECOMING MORE EFFECTIVE TOMORROW THAN YOU ARE TODAY.

Volume 8

OF

THE EFFECTIVENESS GUIDE

BY

EDWARD J. MURPHY

Never STOP Learning!

Copyright © 2012 by

The Effectiveness Institute (TEI)

All rights reserved. No part of this book may be reproduced, distributed, or transmitted in any form or by any means without the prior written permission of TEI.

Volume 8, 2021, Amazon Paperback Version, from *The Effectiveness Institute Series* of 11 Books. Version 6, LU: 2/22.

TheEffectivenessInstitute.com.

BISAC: Business & Economics / Leadership

Printed in The United States of America

9781544824178

WHAT OTHERS SAY ABOUT
The Effectiveness Institute

"I highly recommend the books from The Effectiveness Institute as texts for new leaders and a review for seasoned leaders - as a reminder of what they should be doing. These books are unique because they're replete with valuable information that you can actually learn today and use tomorrow. If you want to become absolutely essential to any organization, these books are for you."

- Dennis D. Cavin
Lieutenant General, US Army (Retired)
Vice President Army and Missile Defense Programs
Lockheed Martin, Corporate Business Development

"I recommend the books from The Effectiveness Institute because Ed Murphy doesn't theorize; he draws on his extensive experience from many years of service in the US Military and from working as an Executive Coach in Corporate America. His keen insights and practical advice make these books required reading for anyone trying to negotiate the maze of organizational chaos."

- Lee Lacy
Assistant Professor
US Army Warfighter Book
Command and General Staff College

"The books from The Effectiveness Institute will help you become more effective at work and in life. They will also help you unlock your potential and direct your team to greater success. I highly recommend these books."

- Lance Revo
Principal Engineering Design Specialist
Cyber Security at AREVA NP

I DEDICATE THIS BOOK TO

My Youngest Daughter

and

Gifted Esthetician.

TRISHA LYNNE MURPHY

"Trisha, since I won't be around to help you, I've decided to let this book speak for me. May my words help you either avoid or abate the mistakes, failures, and problems I've encountered throughout my lifetime. I pray that you might find true and lasting joy, which can only come by serving others. Do something meaningful with your life. Pay it forward and help others rise. Know that I love you and your wonderful family always."

Other Books From
THE EFFECTIVENESS INSTITUTE

Here are the eleven volumes from *The Effectiveness Institute*, one for each Core Competencies of Effectiveness:

VOLUME 1: The Power of FOLLOWERSHIP

VOLUME 2: The Power of DELEGATING

VOLUME 3: The Power of PLANNING

VOLUME 4: The Power of ORGANIZING

VOLUME 5: The Power of COMMUNICATING

VOLUME 6: The Power of PROBLEM-SOLVING

VOLUME 7: The Power of AWARENESS

VOLUME 8: The Power of TRAINING

VOLUME 9: The Power of MOTIVATION

VOLUME 10: The Power of CHARACTER

All the above books are available at *Amazon.com*

Never STOP Learning!

This page is intentionally left blank.

CONTENTS

PREFACE	- 9 -
INTRODUCTION	- 11 -
1 THE POWER OF TRAINING	- 15 -
2 BY CONDUCTING SENSITIVITY TRAINING	- 19 -
3 BY KNOWING WHAT EVERY BOSS NEEDS TO SURVIVE	- 21 -
4 BY SELECTING TEAM MEMBER TASKS	- 23 -
5 BY CREATING LEARNING OBJECTIVES	- 25 -
6 BY CREATING A PLAYBOOK	- 27 -
7 BY SELECTING THE BEST TIME TO TRAIN	- 31 -
8 BY USING THE ADULT LEARNING MODEL	- 33 -
9 BY TRAINING-THE-TRAINER	- 35 -
10 BY USING ROLE-PLAYING	- 37 -
11 BY CREATING A LEARNING ENVIRONMENT	- 39 -
12 BY CONDUCTING AN AFTER-ACTION REVIEW	- 41 -
13 BY REVIEWING PERFORMANCE	- 43 -
14 BY CONTINUING EDUCATION AND TRAINING	- 45 -
15 BY GIVING AND RECEIVING FEEDBACK	- 47 -
16 BY SETTING GOALS	- 49 -
17 BY COMMITTING TO PURPOSE	- 51 -
18 BY OVERCOMING FEAR	- 53 -
19 BY EXPANDING YOUR LEARNING ZONE	- 59 -
20 BY DEMONSTRATING COURAGE	- 61 -
21 BY MAKING A PRESENTATION	- 63 -
22 BY BUILDING EFFECTIVE TEAMS	- 71 -
23 BY BUILDING TRUST	- 73 -
24 BY BUILDING CONSENSUS WITH A TEAM	- 77 -
25 BY COACHING FOR PEAK PERFORMANCE	- 83 -
26 BY MANAGING RISK	- 87 -

27	BY CONDUCTING A RISK ASSESSMENT	- 91 -
28	BY MITIGATING THE RISK TO BAD SITUATIONS	- 93 -
29	BY CREATING CONTINGENCY PLANS	- 95 -
30	BY CONDUCTING A REHEARSAL	- 99 -
31	BY CONDUCTING A BRAINSTORMING SESSION	- 101 -
32	BY ELIMINATING UNRESOLVED ISSUES	- 103 -
33	BY ANTICIPATING CONSEQUENCES AND EFFECTS	- 107 -
34	BY DEMONSTRATING GOOD JUDGMENT	- 111 -
35	BY KNOWING WHEN TO ACT, WAIT OR WALK AWAY	- 113 -
36	BY LEARNING FROM MISTAKES AND FAILURE	- 117 -
37	BY ASSESSING PERFORMANCE	- 123 -
38	BY CREATING MORE EFFECTIVE TEAM MEMBERS	- 129 -
APPENDIX A:	USE INTERNAL COMPETITION	- 133 -
B	CREATE A PLAN OF ACTION	- 135 -
C	CREATE A DECISION PAPER	- 139 -
D	REAL WORLD PROBLEM-SOLVING EXAMPLE	- 141 -
E	"DON'T FORGIT NOTHIN"	- 149 -
F	TAKE IMMEDIATE ACTION	- 153 -
G	USE CRITICAL REASONING & CREATIVE THINKING	- 157 -
H	ASSESS YOUR ACCOUNTABILITY	- 159 -
ACKNOWLEDGMENTS		- 165 -
ABOUT THE AUTHOR		- 167 -
CONCLUSION		- 169 -

PREFACE

I'm often asked, "What does the picture mean on the cover of your book?"

This picture is a metaphor for the dilemma young people face when coming from school to the world-of-work.

They're unprepared, do not have the right tools, the right motivation, nor any clue of what's most important to every employer on the planet.

The cover image shows a young man rowing a boat in the fog. If you look closer, you'll notice that the boat is too small for the person in it. You can tell because one side of the boat is dipping so low in the water that it's almost taking on water. You can also tell that he has little experience in a boat because the other side of the boat is way out of the water because his weight is not evenly distributed.

He is also rowing in dense fog. He cannot see where he's going. The further he gets from shore; he cannot turn around and head back because he has no idea from which direction he came.

Finally, since he's not wearing a flotation device, he's assuming he won't have to swim. You know where assumptions take you, right? He is totally unprepared.

He didn't plan his trip, nor is he prepared to deal with the consequences of what lies ahead. He is, or will soon be, lost and at the mercy of nature.

Such is the fate of young workers today.

In today's job market, there's a huge skills gap between graduation and the first day on the job. As a result, young people lack the job skills needed to "hit-the-ground-running" and find themselves in dead-end, menial, minimum-wage jobs, trading time for money just to put food on the table. And it will take them decades before they're effective enough to *add value* to any employer. What a waste!

How do I know that? I know it because I've spent 20+ years of my life as an executive coach, working with hundreds of business executives and small business owners, seeking the answer to this simple question:

Why are some people more effective than others?

What do they think, say, and do that made them more effective?

During that time, I was privileged to work with some of the most exceptional men and women in America. Through their example, I learned the true definition of effectiveness by documenting what they did, how they did it, and most importantly, how they made people feel. What you'll find here is the result of my years of research.

Today, my purpose in life is to help you navigate the world-of-work, maximize your true career potential, and become more effective and successful at work and in life.

ENJOY!

INTRODUCTION

"Confidence comes from discipline and training."
- Robert Kiyosaki

This book is about ***Training****!*

Training is your ability to effectively train your team members for the future by increasing their performance, unleashing their potential, and encouraging their professional development.

Training is also one of these eleven Core Competencies of your effectiveness and success at work and in life.

Followership, Delegating, Planning, Organizing, Communicating, Problem-Solving, Decision-Making, Awareness, Training, Motivating and Character.

This book is for everyone in the workforce who reports to another person for their work assignments, including employees working for an employer and small business owners, entrepreneurs, and the self-employed working for customers, clients, or patients.

Simply stated, this book is for you regardless of your occupation, position, or level of authority.

You may not realize that *Training* is one the most powerful and underrated transferrable skills in business today. If you have any desire to consistently produce excellent results and sustain those results, you need to assume a more active role in the training of your team members.

If you're responsible for your team's results, you're responsible for how they achieve those results. Now, you're responsible for the process of achieving those results and how to make them better.

And that process should include setting goals, selecting team member tasks, creating learning objectives, creating playbooks for your team members, selecting the best time to train, using the Adult Training Model, role-playing, and train-the-trainer, creating a learning environment, conducting After-Action Reviews, reviewing performance, and building effective teams for the future - all of which are addressed in this book.

Your goal is to train your team members to become more effective and successful by increasing their performance, unleashing their potential, and encouraging their professional development.

Without these abilities, you'll be wasting your career sitting on the sidelines, watching others move ahead while wondering why?

I speak from 24 years as a US Army Officer and 20 years as an Executive Coach in Corporate America in Seattle, San Diego, Kansas City, and Phoenix.

As an Executive Coach, I was blessed to work with some of America's most successful men and women, including hundreds of business executives, teams, and small business owners. I documented what they said, did, how they did it, what worked and what didn't. But, most importantly, I documented how they made people feel.

As a result, I learned that the most effective and successful people stood out because they were able to do these two things better than anyone else:

- First, to consistently produce excellent results.
- Second, to add value to those who helped produce those results.

This book will enhance your ability to do both.

The fact is that you may be the top producer, but if you haven't added value to those who helped you, especially your boss, you'll never become effective or successful, period.

What new skills or abilities have you acquired in the last twelve months? What contributions have you made to your current position since this time last year?

And, most of all, what are you doing about it?

This book is unique because it:

- Gives you the most actionable tactics, techniques, and tools needed to consistently produce excellent results.
- Teaches you the best practices used every day by the most effective and successful people in their field, which you were never taught in school.

- Provides you with step-by-step instructions explaining what and how things should be done that you won't find anywhere in academia or Corporate America to help you maximize your true potential.
- Contains everything you want to know about *Training*, plus everything you didn't realize you need to know about how *Training* enhances your effectiveness and success in business.

I know that by learning, using, and sharing the best practices found here, you'll be well on your way to becoming more effective and successful.

Remember, no matter how good you think you are; you can always be better.

So, what are you waiting for? You have too much to lose by not taking a more active role in your Professional Development. When you're ready to *elevate-your-game* to the next level, join us on this incredible *Journey of Discovery*.

Also, if you feel this information could help someone else, please let them know. If it turns out to make a difference in their life, they'll be forever grateful to you, as will I.

Never STOP Learning!

Ed

Founder of *The Effectiveness Institute*
email: ed.murphy77@gmail.com

Stop wishing you were better and do something about it today!

This page is intentionally left blank.

1
THE POWER OF TRAINING

*"It's not the will to win that matters – everyone has that.
It's the will to prepare to win that matters."
– Coach Paul "Bear" Bryant*

This book will give you a far better understanding of *Training*, its definition, importance, and how to do it successfully.

Training is your ability to effectively train your team members for the future by increasing their performance, unleashing their potential, and encouraging their professional development.

Training your team members is the best way to add value to all who help you produce your results. If you have any desire to consistently produce excellent results and sustain those results, you need to assume a more active role in the training of your team members. If you're responsible for their results, you're responsible for how they achieve those results. You're responsible for the process of achieving those results and how to make them better.

Here, you'll learn to use the most actionable *tactics, techniques, and tools* needed to enhance your ability to train others for the future. As an executive coach for over 20 years, I know what your boss and customers expect, especially regarding your effectiveness and success at work.

Effective people know that their ability to train others is critical to their effectiveness and success at work. By learning, using, and sharing these *best practices*, you'll be well on your way to becoming the one person who adds the greatest value to the team - making you essential.

Also, to make this book easier to understand, I'll use the term "boss" instead of leader, employer, or customer. I do this because if you're an employee, your boss is your employer. And if you're self-employed or a small business owner, your boss is your customer, client, or patient.

This means that you'll always be working for a boss – whoever pays you for your products or services.

This also means that you'll always be a follower of someone – whoever pays you for your work.

So, let's get to work!

Why should you train your team members?

Effective people know how critical training is for their team members. You probably never thought of yourself as a trainer, but unconsciously you're training them every day by your example, by what you say and do, and what you fail to say and do. I'll bet you thought that training was the responsibility of your boss or Human Resources. Yes, they play a role in training, but so do you. Why? Because you have the most to lose if your team fails to consistently produce excellent results.

That's why *The Effectiveness Institute* is so powerful! Its eleven volumes constitute the best-in-class knowledge, wisdom, and advice on both personal and team effectiveness. It contains the most important fundamental knowledge, skill, and ability to maximize your true potential and isn't found anywhere in academia or Corporate America.

How can you train your team members?

The most effective way is by example. As you learn, use, and share what you'll learn here, you can make a difference.

- You can assign a team member as the primary trainer (*Train-the-Trainer (Chapter 9)* for certain critical tasks by using the *Adult Learning Model (Chapter 8)*.

- You can set aside the time to train your team and use scenarios or simulations via *Role-Playing (Chapter 10)*.

- You can make assignments to members by asking them to use the *Problem-Solving Process* (PSP) to resolve problems (Appendix D), write a decision paper (Appendix C), or make a presentation (Chapter 21).

What are the three main types of Business Training?

- **Compulsory Training,** like Safety, Security, Code of Conduct, and Standard Operating Procedures. Which may require annual testing and certification.
- **On-the-Job Training,** like receptionist, help desk, customer care, and other training related to their duties.
- **Professional Development Training,** like delegating, planning, problem-solving, and decision-making.

Effective people know that speaking to make a presentation means speaking to a group of people for these three purposes: to Persuade, Inform, or Instruct.

What are the three basic types of Business Presentations?

1. Speaking to Persuade.

Speaking to Persuade is your ability to guide someone through a field of ignorance to where there's enough understanding to make a logical choice to do what's in their best interest.

2. Speaking to Inform.

Speaking to Inform is your ability to provide information in a manner that's easily understood, compelling and convincing, free of errors in grammar, mechanics, and usage, and clear, concise, organized, and to the point.

This could include revealing a new plan going forward, providing the status of a project or activity, or speaking to inspire and motivate.

3. Speaking to Instruct.

Speaking to Instruct is your ability to create more effective team members for the future by improving their performance, unleashing their potential, and encouraging their personal and professional development throughout their working life.

This page is intentionally left blank.

2
BY CONDUCTING SENSITIVITY TRAINING

"I'm not concerned with your liking or disliking me...
All I ask is that you respect me as a human being."
- Jackie Robinson

Sensitivity in the workplace ensures that everyone is treated with respect and kindness, regardless of who they are. It involves learning how to be respectful and consider the perspectives of others.

By conducting Sensitivity Training Annually

Sensitivity training:
- Is about respecting each member as an equal and as a human being.
- Involves identifying what is likely to be offensive and developing the ability to sincerely apologize when feelings are hurt.
- Includes race, culture, gender, sensitivity, and tolerance.
- Teaches:
  - ✓ Diverse group characteristics and definitions, such as cultural, disability, gender, age, and sexual orientation.
  - ✓ How to identify their conflict resolution style and how their style might differ from others.
  - ✓ How to engage in perspective-taking so that it's easier for them to appreciate another point of view and come to a mutual understanding.
  - ✓ Sexual Harassment Prevention and EEOC Courses.
  - ✓ American Disabilities Act (ADA) and Multiculturalism and Conflict Resolution.
  - ✓ Bullying in the Workplace and *Keeping the Peace*.
  - ✓ Sexual Orientation and Gender Identity in the Workplace.

Federal laws prohibit discrimination and harassment in the workplace based on age, sex, race, religion, national origin, disability, pregnancy, and genetic information. Some state and local laws protect even more.

Training members on how to prevent workplace discrimination and harassment is nothing less than essential to long-term success.

For me, any form of discrimination, resulting in meanness, unfairness, or abusive behavior is hateful, despicable, and unacceptable for any reason.

Not only can workplace discrimination and harassment affect member productivity, but they can also divert resources from the organization's real focus (a distraction). In addition, unacceptable behavior can also become a liability to your company because of discrimination or harassment lawsuits.

By Apologizing with Remorse

Why is it so hard to say you're sorry or admit a mistake? The answer is simple; you're letting your fear and pride get in your way of doing the right thing.

When you hurt someone's feelings or your behavior was unacceptable, have the moral courage to apologize, say you're sorry, what you're sorry for, offer no excuse, and don't do it again.

Why no excuses? Making excuses diminishes your sincerity and makes you sound like you're trying to hide behind your excuse. You're human, and humans make mistakes. Express your sincere remorse, not guilt. Guilt is acknowledging your unacceptable behavior, while remorse is regretting your actions and taking steps to undo the damage. When your finish, look down, say nothing, and wait for a response. The other person doesn't have to forgive you, but you need to forgive yourself and move forward. Guilt leads to destructive tendencies, while remorse leads to constructive actions. To be remorseful, you must accept the guilt first.

When you make a mistake, have the moral courage to admit it, fix it, and learn from it.

Being *in-charge* is about making decisions, and sometimes your decisions will make you unpopular. This is why doing the right thing can be difficult. Stay calm, stay focused, and listen to input from your team. Then, communicate honestly as to the reasoning behind your decision.

3
BY KNOWING WHAT EVERY BOSS NEEDS TO SURVIVE

> *"It takes half your life before you discover life is a do-it-yourself project."*
> *- Napoleon Hill*

Effective bosses need effective *followers who can resolve problems and achieve goals (Chapter 16). And any effective follower knows how to turn any assignment (a problem, goal, event, or activity) into a simple project that you can easily manage.

As far as your boss is concerned, your effectiveness or value-added is a function of your ability to successfully manage projects. And you don't need to be a *certified project manager* to manage projects successfully. All you need is a basic understanding of a few tactics, techniques, and tools, which you'll learn here.

The better you get at managing projects, the more value you bring to your boss. And for every project, you'll encounter obstacles along the way. All you need to do is to convert each obstacle into another project and make it go away.

What's a Project?

I define a project as an assignment that requires the effort of others. Anything you can do yourself is a task and not a project. So, whenever you get stuck at work, just realize there's a simple way to re-frame anything into a project to get things moving again.

What's a Plan of Action?

Every project needs a good *Plan of Action*, even if it's only a mental plan or a sketch on the back of a napkin. Any good *Plan of Action (POA)* format (Appen A) has at least six components:

Objective: Who, What, Where, When, and Why (Appen A)?

Methods: How will we accomplish this Objective (Appen A)?

Timetable: Planning backward from today, how will we use the time available to plan and prepare (Appen A and Chaps 6-7)?

*To learn more about **Followership**, available at **Amazon.com**, see page 5.

Resources: What will you need (Appen A)?

Unresolved Issues: What are all the things (questions, unknowns, concerns, shortfalls, obstacles, or problems) that could slow or stop your progress (Appen. A, Chap. 16)?

Risk: What could *reasonably-go-wrong* and how can they be *mitigated* (Appen A and Chaps 24-29)?

If you don't know certain information, still list the category, but show a TBD (To Be Determined). For example, if you don't know the end time, show, End time: TBD.

What's a Project's Life Cycle?

Every project has at least four phases: Planning, Preparing (before), Executing (during), and Assessing (during).

Here's a *Gannt Chart* showing the four phases of a one-day project that begins in 30-days:

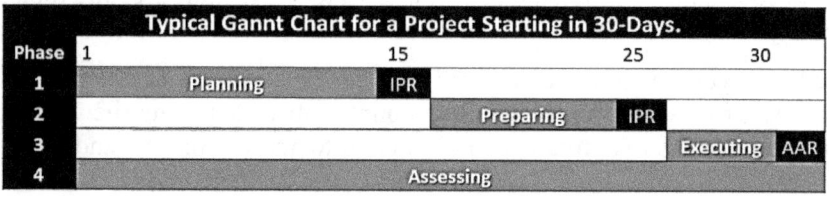

Notice that the *Assessing Phase* is conducted continuously throughout the project and is formalized using two *In-Progress Reviews* (or IPRs), numerous *Project Updates*, and one *After-Action Review* (or AAR) (Chap 34).

4
BY SELECTING TEAM MEMBER TASKS

"I hated every minute of training, but I said, 'Don't quit. Suffer now and live the rest of your life as a champion."
- Muhammad Ali

Have you ever noticed that just by the time your members learn what they need to learn, which could take a few years, they somehow end up forgetting what they learned or move somewhere else?

This is why effective people have cyclic, focused, and dynamic training program already in place.

What's a Task?

A task is a clearly defined and measurable activity accomplished by a member and teams. It's the lowest behavioral level in a job or unit that is performed for its own sake. Therefore, the most important things to consider when designing each task is that it:

- Must be specific, observable, measurable, and usually has a definite beginning and end.
- May support or be supported by other tasks.
- Have only one action.
- Is described using only one action verb.
- Is normally performed in a short time.

Here are the most important tasks your members should be able to perform:

Group 1: How to create a Document: Includes how to create a Plan of Action, Contingency Plans, Mitigation Plans, Opinion Paper, Decision Paper, Decision Matrix, Authorization Matrix, Decision Points, Decision Support Templates, Dashboard, and Timetable.

Group 2: How to make a Presentation: Includes how to conduct a Decision Briefing, Backbriefing, Briefback, Sales Meeting, Training Session, Situation Report, and Project Update.

Group 3: How to conduct a Meeting: Includes how to conduct a Problem-Solving Process, Brainstorming, Risk Assessment, After Action Review, Quarterly Progress Briefing, Problem Resolution Meeting, In-Progress Review, and Rehearsal.

Group 4: Other Skills: Includes how to anticipate problems, lead, plan, organize, resolve conflict, decide, delegate, inspire, motivate, encourage, direct, research, follow, anticipate, train, recognize, respond, reprimand, budget, praise, listen, negotiate, coach, provide feedback, improve customer service, schedule, staff a document, collaborate, build consensus, track, supervise, follow up, follow-through, communicate, coordinate, facilitate, inspect, correct, set standards, measure results, make improvements, solve problems, exploit opportunities, assess performance, and administer punishment.

All the key tasks you'll want your team members to perform are contained within this book. Based on the functions your members perform, which tasks do you want them to master?

What are Collective Tasks?

Are there some tasks that more than one member must perform? If so, you have a collective or team task. Collective tasks describe the team's desired performance under actual operational conditions and are derived from unit goals and assignments. These tasks are normally managed separately from individual tasks. They are clearly defined, discrete, and measurable actions that require *organized team performance and lead to accomplishing the team's goal.

Caution: Be careful with internal competition (Appendix A).

What's the Proficiency Cycle?

A Proficiency Cycle is how often you want certain tasks demonstrated to standard to maintain the desired level of proficiency. For example, are there some critical tasks that you want each member to periodically demonstrate their proficiency (quarterly, semi-annually, or annually) like safety, security, driving, lifesaving, or weapons?

*To learn more about *Organizing*, available at **Amazon.com,** see page 5.

5
BY CREATING LEARNING OBJECTIVES

*"Failure comes only when we forget our ideals
and objectives and principles."
- Jawaharlal Nehru*

A Learning Objective is a statement describing what you want a member to do and consists of Terminal and Enabling Learning Objectives.

- **Terminal Learning Objectives (TLOs)** are the big things normally found in the Job Description and should be determined first with the help of your team.
- **Enabling Learning Objectives (ELOs)** must be performed to satisfy each TLO, are subtasks to TLOs, and have three components: Action, Condition, and Standard (ACS):
  - ✓ Action: Lists the action to be performed (using the appropriate action verb).
  - ✓ Condition: Lists the resources and constraints critical to performance.
  - ✓ Standard: Lists the criteria for satisfactory performance (Quantity and Quality) (GO, NO-GO).

Here's an example of a Terminal Learning Objective (TLO) and its three Enabling Learning Objectives (ELO).

TLO #1:
Provide Excellent Customer Service via Helpdesk

Provide excellent customer service via the helpdesk becomes your Terminal Learning Objective (TLO), right from their Job Description. The Enabling Learning Objectives (ELO) contribute to the accomplishment of this TLO might look like these.

ELO 1:

- Action: Answer the Helpdesk phone.
- Condition: Given a phone and a phone script.

- Standard: Answer phone before the second ring using a script (provided separately).

ELO 2:

- Action: Answer simple customer questions.
- Condition: Given phone, internal SOP, and a simple problem that can be resolved.
- Standard: Answer customer questions completely and courteously or redirect their call in less than one minute.

ELO 3:

- Action: Answer complex customer questions.
- Condition: Given phone, internal SOP, and a problem you cannot solve in 2 minutes.
- Standard: Answer customer questions completely and courteously. If unable to solve their problem, record their name and phone number and tell them you will call them with an answer. Get back to them with an answer in one hour or less.

Without having an Action, Condition, and Standard, how will your team members know what you want them to do and how well you want it done?

6
BY CREATING A PLAYBOOK

"Finding good players is easy.
Getting them to play as a team is another story."
- Casey Stengel

Every team member should have a *Playbook* consisting of either a three-ring binder or its digital equivalent.

A Playbook is a collection of the most important processes, procedures, and policies, needed by a member to perform their job.

As a minimum, each *Playbook* should contain:

- Their duties, responsibilities, expectations, constraints, authority, projects, and standards.
- Organizational charts and diagrams and Standard Operating Procedures.
- Rules of Conduct and Ethics and Training Actions, Conditions, and Standards.
- A listing of all assignments he has completed and working on.
- Formats for standard documents, like a Decision Paper or a Decision-Making Process.
- Usernames, passwords, phone numbers, combinations, and URLs.
- Operating instructions for all the systems for which he's responsible.
- All recurring events, like weekly, monthly, quarterly, and annual.
- A copy of his boss's *Philosophy of Serving*.
- A listing of any tools or equipment for which he's responsible.
- A list of do's and don't (or expectations) for meetings and internal communication.

Without having some form of *Playbook* for each team member, where do you want them to go to find this information? It should be used (or exchanged) when a new member transitions in or out of your unit. *Playbooks* will make your in-processing and transitioning process easier.

They also ensure your team members are empowered to do their best work moving forward. Every company needs a *Playbook* to scale successfully.

What are the Advantages of a Playbook?

A *Playbook* helps:

- Teams stay aligned, and members stay accountable.
- The company scale successfully.
- Anyone on the team can fill any position.
- Keep the business running smoothly.
- Explain how the business does what it does, down to each role and responsibility.

Playbooks also permit members to *cross-train* to help offset the effects of absenteeism and turnover. Without a *Playbook*, this leaves members guessing the best, safest, or most efficient way to do something. If your members have to guess what to do, this will cost you time and money.

How do you create a Playbook?

Here are the most important steps to create a *Playbook*:

Step 1. List: Ask each team member to list every important task for which they're responsible.

Step 2. Consolidate: Consolidate the tasks from each team member to ensure there are no duplications of duties and responsibilities.

Step 3. Alignment: How do these tasks relate to their boss's goals?

Step 4. Objective: What's the objective for each task. Who else is involved, what, when, where, and why?

Step 5. Method: Ask each member to create a step-by-step outline of how each task should be performed. Pictures, diagrams, and examples are helpful.

Step 6. Risk: What's the probability and impact of what you could lose and what could *reasonably-go-wrong*?

Step 7. Timetable: When do you start, and how long will it take?

Step 8. Resources needed: What will you need?

Step 9. Unresolved Issues: Capture and eliminate any question, unknown, concern, shortfall, obstacle, or problem that could slow or stop your progress (Chapter 32).

Step 10. Update: Every quarter, update all *Playbooks* by looking for opportunities to improve how you do things. As you find better practices, you'll need to update the *Playbook (Chapter 6)*.

This page is intentionally left blank.

7
BY SELECTING THE BEST TIME TO TRAIN

"Time and tide wait for no man."
- Geoffrey Chaucer.

The biggest training problem bosses face is finding the best time to train their members.

Here's a Technique:
Schedule training for every Wednesday from 1-3 PM and make it mandatory for all.

Mandatory means no one schedules non-emergency medical appointments, travel, or other voluntary absences during training (except vacation). Next, require that your team members conduct their training on subjects they feel they need or train on a recurring basis (month, quarter, or semi-annual) like this example.

Here's an example of a Cyclic Unit Training Schedule:

Which Wednesday? / Subjects / Notes

    1st of month / Problem-Solving / Includes Decision-Making

    2nd / Written communications / Includes email

    3rd / Verbal communications / Includes Backbriefings

    4th / Collaboration / Include Consensus Building

    5th / Brainstorming

Ensure your boss and his boss recognize and approve that Wednesday PM is mandatory training time for your unit and not to schedule any activities during this time.

Only if you protect this time will you be able to train your members. If some of your members are routinely on the road during the week, arrange their online training and be available 24/7. Dental and medical practices close their offices for a half-day per week or per month.

This page is intentionally left blank.

8
BY USING THE ADULT LEARNING MODEL

"The mediocre teacher tells. The good teacher explains. The superior teacher demonstrates. The great teacher inspires."
- William Arthur Ward

Effective people know that the best way to train their members is by using the *Adult Learning Model*.

The Adult Learning Model is a four-phase process of training adults where each member must physically demonstrate a skill to standard to maintain proficiency on a work-related task.

An example might include annual weapons qualification for a law enforcement officer.

Here's a detailed look at each of the four phases of the Adult Learning Model:

- **Phase 1: Explaining.** Here, the trainer explains the task she wants the member to perform and why the task is important, like completing a report, processing an order, or helping a client with a problem.

    The three components of a task include:

    - ✓ Action: What action must be performed?
    - ✓ Condition: What resources and constraints are critical to their performance?
    - ✓ Standard: The criteria for satisfactory performance, including quantity/quality.

    Explains the **Go, No-Go** standard.

- **Phase 2: Demonstrating.** This is where the trainer demonstrates the task to standard while the members observe.

- **Phase 3: Practicing.** This is where the trainer permits the member to practice as much as needed. Then, the trainer provides feedback and encouragement. For example, if the member didn't perform the task to standard, the trainer provides feedback and encouragement and asks the member to repeat the task until the member can complete the task to standard before testing.
- **Phase 4: Testing.** When the member is ready to be tested, testing begins while the trainer observes. If it's a written task, she doesn't have to stand over the trainee while he writes. Instead, she reviews the final product.
    - ✓ If the member receives a **Go** on the task, the trainer records the Go, the date and informs the member when the next qualifying test will be conducted (annual or semi-annual).
    - ✓ If the member receives a **No-Go** on the task, the trainer explains what the member did wrong and schedules a retest. Again, ensure retests are as discrete as possible.

Here's a true story

"Joe volunteered to be a member of a security detail at a political fundraising event. Each security person was given instructions on turning on and using the two-way radios they were each provided. However, no one asked them to do a radio check or demonstrate their ability to talk on the radio before they were posted to their positions. As a result, several radios didn't work, and no one knew how to talk on the radio, which call signs belonged to whom, how to report where they were, or how to respond if something happened."

I used this story to illustrate the value of Phases 3 and 4. Each member needs the chance to demonstrate that they perform the task to standard. Telling someone isn't enough. Showing someone is a little better. But telling, showing, and asking them to perform the task is the only way you'll ever know that they got it. This is what makes the *Adult Learning Model* far superior to other methods.

So, what's the Big Deal?

The biggest problem with training today is the failure to provide a standard of performance and conduct Phases 3 and 4. If you skip these phases, how do you know if the member can truly execute the task? In addition, members need feedback that they've done the task to standard to build their confidence.

9
BY
TRAINING-THE-TRAINER

"Confidence comes from discipline and training."
- Robert Kiyosaki.

This can be a delegated task or a long-term additional duty.

Train-the-Trainer means that one team member is the primary trainer and tester for a specific critical skill like firearms proficiency.

This is where each member is assigned a specific task to teach (when new members join the team) and to qualify (when current members reach their qualification period (annual or semi-annual). To truly own a skill, you must freely give it away by teaching it to others.

Adults learn best by doing, not by watching, reading, or by being shown how to do it!

According to **Aaron Hurst**, Co-Founder & CEO, *Imperative*, there is a strong business case in favor of *"Train-the-Trainer" (or Peer Coaching)*.

> *"As it turns out, the career advice I have been dispensing all this time may be wrong. When asked what to look for in a new job, I often tell people to focus their attention on the manager: What can you learn from them? Imperative is releasing some new research this quarter, which sheds light on a new workplace truth. We asked a representative sample of the US workforce, "Do you learn more from their managers or your peers?" 20% said they learned more from their managers. 53% said they learned more from their peers, and 27% said they learned equally from their peers and managers."*

Why do people learn more from their peers?

> *"This means 80% of people learn as much or more from their peers as they do from their managers. Not only does this mean I was giving the wrong advice, but it also means that our way of thinking about work and career development is upside down. This is yet another example of how work is changing. The issues with hierarchical organizations and command and control cultures have been well documented.*

But, even with this knowledge, we continue to apply an old model to career development and learning."

1. Psychological Safety

"Our managers are also responsible for our compensation and career path in most organizations, leading to higher stakes for employees. This is more likely to bring negative emotions into the learning experience. To learn, we need to take risks and be vulnerable, which is much easier with a peer.

2. Relevance of Information

Most of our learning is focused on the immediate performance of our jobs. Our peers may be more likely to have the relevant knowledge and experience top of mind than our managers.

3. Adult Learning

The top source of learning at work is gained through experiential learning: doing on-the-job tasks. Experiential learning has been estimated to be 70% of learning. Who are we doing our day-to-day work with? Our peers.

4. Reflection

When we learn new things, either from consuming information or experience, we are much more likely to have that learning stick if we reflect on it. Peers provide a natural resource for reflection. What did you think of that meeting? How do we need to act on that new information? Why do you think that didn't work? Through this process, we begin to create new approaches and actively test them in the real world.

5. Availability

Peers have more availability than managers. In a poll from Interact Harris poll, 52% of employees reported that their bosses don't have the time to meet with them. Peer coaching allows employees to have the one-to-one interactions they crave and are not receiving.

6. Reciprocity

We feel more comfortable asking for advice when we can return the favor. Peer learning creates reciprocity that is less likely in a manager-employee relationship."

10
BY USING
ROLE-PLAYING

*"What I hear, I forget. What I see, I remember.
What I do, I understand."*
- Confucius

How can you add realism and meaning to any training situation?

Role-Playing is a training technique used to replicate an actual situation by a trainer acting out a simulated situation to assess a trainee's behavior as if the situation were real.

Role-Playing can be used to train a member how to interview a new hire (what would you do in this situation), resolve customer problems, and assess a group's ability to collaborate and achieve consensus. Your options are limited only by your imagination.

What's needed to effectively use Role-Playing?

- **An Actor:** Person presenting the situation.
- **A Trainee:** Person responding to the situation.

    An Enabling Learning Objective (ELO):

    ✓ Action: An expected and realistic simulated situation or problem

    ✓ Condition: Actual conditions under which the action is expected to be performed

    ✓ Standard: An expected outcome or result - what the boss and organization expect.

- **Feedback:** Provided at the end by team members and the boss.

A team member is selected at random every week. This training, if conducted every week, will strengthen both the member and the team.

Sometimes the actor can be the boss. The member's task is to respond to a simulated situation using common sense and the training and tools provided.

And when you're finished, you can select another team member at random to assess the member's performance before you offer your assessment.

Example:

> "Bob wanted to enhance his team's ability to resolve problems on their own without his help. However, he knew that to be effective; he needed to conduct this training every week with a different team member as a facilitator.
>
> - *The first week, Bob gave each team member a copy of the Problem-Solving Process and discussed each step and how it should be used (Appendix D).*
> - *In the second week, Bob led the first group Problem-Solving session using a simulated situation.*
> - *In the third week, Bob selected one member at random to facilitate the team using a simulated situation. At the end of this training session, Bob asked another member to assess what happened. Then, Bob offered his assessment.*
> - *Every week after that, Bob repeated the process until he was satisfied that his team knew what to do. Bob conducted this exercise every year because this was a critical task for his team."*

You are preparing your team members to become more effective tomorrow than they are today.

11
BY CREATING A LEARNING ENVIRONMENT

"One of the main focuses of my training sessions is to help individuals find their unique voices in the learning process."
- Joshua Waitzkin

Effective people apply and train all their members on the *11 Core Competencies of Effectiveness*. They create a learning environment where members can feel free to express their opinions, discuss their successes and failures, make mistakes, and ask questions without fear of ridicule or punishment. Adults learn more from their peers than they will from you or any book. And that's the way it should be!

What are the most important conditions for an ideal Learning Environment?

- **Confidentiality:** What happens in the classroom - stays in the classroom! Every member needs the freedom to make mistakes and to learn from them.

- **Inclusiveness:** Every attempt should be made to include everyone in all activities because everyone is important. Everyone's opinion is important.

- **Respect:** Everyone should be treated with respect and kindness, regardless of their age, position, or title.

- **Sharing:** Everyone must share their experiences. Members learn more from their peers than they ever will from a book or you. We all learn best from our mistakes and the mistakes of others. Always close the lesson by summarizing, *"What did we learn today?"*

What are the most important training warnings?

- Don't scold, embarrass, or demean anyone for any reason. You don't have to agree with what was said or done. You're the traffic cop to make sure everyone is civil.

- Avoid being openly judgmental. Your job is to ask questions rather than make judgments. Instead, become a more effective active listener drawing out the best from each member. What are you sensing?

- Don't announce or discuss a NO-GO in front of other members. You can provide feedback when others are present, but do not tell a member that he received a NO-GO in front of others.

- Don't permit personal attacks on another. Instead, everyone should treat and be treated with respect and kindness.

- Don't permit members to mention another person's name in a negative context.

- In addition to looking for things wrong, look for, and praise what was right and how much improvement was made.

You're looking for improvement, not perfection!

In the end, this entire experience is designed for all those who want to improve themselves. Your job is to guide and encourage them to improve with every lesson without getting in their way!

What other Training Tools can you use?

- **Notebooks:** Provide a blank notebook at the beginning of each training session for each member to write their questions and concerns. At the end of each session, each member turns in their notebook to the trainer. Each member must write something in their notebook before turning it in. After the session, the trainer reads their comments and responds to them in writing for the next session. This is a confidential way for members to ask questions without looking stupid.

- **3 X 5 Cards:** Cards can be given to selected members (asking them to do something or to Role Play) during the training session to add realism and make the ELO more challenging.

- **Group Exercises:** The team could be assigned the Action to conduct a Brainstorming Session, use the Problem-Solving Process (Appendix D), conduct a meeting (IPR, Problem Resolution Meeting, and Quarterly Progress Briefing), or collaborate and build consensus. The only limitations are your imagination.

- **Ask Better Questions:** Ask open-ended questions: Questions that cannot be answered with a YES or NO. Provide mandatory education for all staff about the impact of disrespectful behavior and appropriate professional behavior as defined by the code of conduct.

12
BY CONDUCTING AN AFTER-ACTION REVIEW

"I never teach my pupils; I only attempt to provide the conditions in which they can learn."
- Albert Einstein

How can you enhance your performance and the performance of your team? One way is to use *After-Action Reviews*.

An After-Action Review (AAR) is a professional discussion conducted after an activity, with all members present, seeking ways to consistently improve the way things are done.

AARs should be conducted both during (at the end of each day) and the day after an activity (project, objective, or goal) by measuring the difference between what was supposed to happen (the Plan) vs. what did happen (Behavior and Results). Thus, AARs observe, measure, record, and assess an activity or process from start to finish to examine both the results and the behavior of those involved.

The purpose of an AAR is to:

- Capture and share intuition by asking HOW and WHY questions.
- Attempt to discover WHY things happen and how to get better.
- Help members understand HOW and WHY decisions are made.
- Encourage members to become *self-correcting* and more *aware of how their behavior affects others (Appendix H).
- Capture *Lessons Learned* to integrate into future operations.

Here are the four most important steps to conducting an AAR:

Step 1. The Objective.

Before the activity (project, objective, or goal): What are we trying to achieve? What performance standards and results are desired? Who and what will be observed, and how will it be measured?

*To learn more about *Awareness*, available at **Amazon.com,** see page 5.

Step 2. The Results and Behavior.

During the activity: What happened? What was observed and measured? What are the facts?

Step 3. The Assessment.

After the activity: Did things go as expected? Were there any surprises? If the result wasn't what we expected, what should be started, stopped, or changed to achieve a better result? WHY and HOW did we do what we did?

Step 4. The Lessons Learned.

What did we learn that can help us do better next time?

By using Informal After-Action Reviews

Let's assume that you're the Project Manager for a four-day Trade Show and you have three team members.

The week before the show, you and your boss sat down to discuss the plan and its objective. Why are we attending this show? What's the ideal outcome you'd like to see? How will this outcome be measured? After finishing with your boss, you met with your team and briefed them on the plan. Fast forward to the end of the first day of the show. You assembled your team and asked, what did we learn today that can make us better tomorrow?

One team member said it would have been nice to have some bottled water in our booth. A second member said, we also need a lunch schedule, so everyone has a chance to eat. Also, we're running low on our advertising brochures. You then asked one team member to provide bottled water in the booth every day. Then you asked another member to set up a lunch schedule for each day. And finally, you called your boss and asked him to overnight a bunch of advertising brochures. You also conducted an informal review at the end of each day with the goal of continuous improvement.

The day after the trade show, you gathered your team together and asked if we accomplished our goal? Did everything go as planned? Were there any surprises? What did we learn that could make the next Trade Show better? You then added all comments to your After-Action Report so next year's Trade Show can be even better. How hard was that?

13
BY REVIEWING PERFORMANCE

"What we can control is our performance and our execution, and that's what we're going to focus on."
- Bill Belichick

Formal written reviews are normally given once a year in writing. However, if you wait a year to review the performance of your team members, you have done them a grave disservice.

They all need to know how they're doing, at least quarterly.

One of the most important things you can do is coach your team members to either reinforce their actions/results, redirect their actions, or both.

Here's an example of what you might do.

Team Member Self-Assessment

Performance coaching should start by asking for a self-assessment like:

"John, tell me how you think your unit has been performing."

"Is there any room for improvement?"

"How do you measure their progress, their results vs. the desired outcome?"

"How about a self-assessment; how do you think you're doing?"

"Any room for self-improvement?"

Note: Some organizations even formalize the process by asking members to fill out a written self-assessment before the session.

Boss's Assessment

Phase 1: Present the Positives

Listen carefully, take notes, and ask thoughtful questions. When you begin your assessment, start by saying,

> *"Do you know what I really like about you? You're... "*
>
> Present all the positives.

Phase 2: Discuss things for them to work on

When ready to provide any constructive feedback, start by saying,

> *"There're a few small things I'd like you to work on. ......"*

This way, you reinforce the positive and assign a few small things to work on in the future.

Phase 3: Goal Setting

> *"Let's set some stretch goals for you to meet for our next meeting. What's fair?"*

Now, negotiate his goals; not too easy, but not too hard. You are building him up for success, not failure. Feedback is critical to everyone's development. It helps close the gap between <u>actual</u> and <u>desired</u> performance. Without it, your members are operating in the dark.

Phase 4: Personal Growth

How's your personal growth plan for your career coming? Since achieving your true potential isn't by accident, what intentional actions are you taking to improve your career?

Document the response for the next review. Provide support as needed.

14
BY CONTINUING EDUCATION AND TRAINING

> *"We cannot solve our problems with the same thinking we used when we created them."*
> *- Albert Einstein*

How can you help your team members improve their performance, unleash their potential, and encourage their professional development throughout their working years?

Effective people know the value of further education, technical training, and certifications for themselves and their team members.

If you're not improving yourself, guess what your peers are doing.

Can you read one book a month in your field? Can you take one course, online, every four months? Of course, you can, but will you? The hardest step to continuing your education and technical training is taking the first course. From then on, you're on the escalator to success.

After high school or college, many people have a negative attitude towards further education and training. The truth is that education and training have little to do with a degree, title, or piece of paper. Rather, it has everything to do with whom you become, whom you meet, and what skills you develop along the way. The journey is always more important than the destination.

It's all about the process: whom you become on the inside because of the journey. The character you've developed along the way makes a big difference. Education and training stretch you to become better. You must produce a result to pass. You've been tested and found worthy.

Doesn't your experience count for anything?

> Absolutely! However, you'll need a lot of it - five years or more. Experience can sometimes substitute for education, depending on the boss. You can still get hired. But it's just a lot more difficult. This is the reality of today's job market.

What are your expected lifetime earnings?

According to a 2011 **Georgetown University** study, here are the expected lifetime earnings based on education levels:

Education Level: ($) Lifetime Earnings:

    High School Dropout: $973,000

    High School Diploma: $1.3 Million

    Some College: $1.5 Million

    Associates Degree: $1.7 Million

    Bachelor's Degree: $2.3 Million

    Master's Degree: $2.7 Million

    Doctorate Degree: $3.3 Million

    Professional Degree: $3.6 Million

Why do people hire college graduates?

Education and training produce members who are more confident and patient, have greater clarity of purpose, are more optimistic, have greater expectations of success at tackling challenges, have a stronger sense of perseverance to overcome obstacles, are better at problem-solving, decision-making, creative thinking, quality control, critical reasoning, receiving corrective criticism, meeting deadlines, producing results, researching, collaborating, coordinating, cooperating, written and verbal communications, software, and technology, getting along with others, and getting things done on-time.

If you ran a company and looked for the best people, which group of people would you hire first?

    Group 1: Those tested and found worthy? (College graduates)

    Group 2: Those tested and found wanting? (Never finished)

    Group 3: Those untested? (No college at all)

If you didn't hire from Group 1 first, you're probably not in business to make a profit. If you're in Groups 2 or 3, you'll need the influence of your network to meet business owners (or hiring managers) and convince them you can be counted on to produce the result they need.

15
BY GIVING AND RECEIVING FEEDBACK

"Feedback is the Breakfast of Champions"
- Ken Blanchard

Have you ever worked for someone who seldom told you how you were doing? How did that make you feel? If you're looking to improve your performance or the performance of others, feedback helps to make the adjustments and corrections needed.

What's Feedback?

Feedback is a process of giving constructive suggestions to improve someone's performance, reinforce good behavior, and improve morale and dedication to doing their jobs.

The goal of feedback is to identify the gap between desired and actual performance (for results and behavior) of members, teams, units, and systems) and to close the gap ASAP.

If you don't receive feedback, ask for it; not only from your boss but others.

Feedback can occur anytime but normally comes during audits, performance-oriented training, performance appraisals and reviews, shareholders' meetings, marketing research, 360-degree feedback, peak performance coaching, visits and observations, on-site inspections, surveys, meetings, and *After-Action Reviews*.

What's the Feedback Loop for Human Performance?

Here are the most important steps of the *Feedback Loop*.

Step 1: Evidence: The performance must be measured, recorded, and assessed.

Step 2: Relevance: Feedback must be relayed to the member in a context that makes sense.

Step 3: Consequence: Feedback must illuminate a path to improvement.

Step 4: Action: Members must change their <u>actual</u> performance to come closer to the <u>desired</u> performance.

Then, that new performance can be re-measured, and the feedback loop can run once more, every action stimulating new performance that moves the member closer to the <u>desired</u> performance.

How do you give Feedback?

If you fail to provide periodic and specific feedback to your members, your silence will speak louder than words. It's your job to let them know how they're doing.

- If your feedback is **positive**, share it with everyone publicly.
- If your feedback is **negative or a correction** (like someone failed to meet a), do so privately. Take a moment to ensure the member knew the correct standard and didn't have a good reason for doing (or failing to do) what he did.

However, giving someone your **opinion** doesn't constitute feedback unless they act on your suggestion and thus cause you to revise your opinion.

How do you receive Feedback?

When you receive feedback, you get to decide how you'll respond and if you'll use it to become more effective.

Feedback is often perceived as a euphemism for criticism. If you just "blow it off," you'll never get any better. You don't have to agree. Initially, you won't. However, arguing or being defensive sends the wrong message.

Humble yourself! Remember, no matter how painful, you need the feedback because you'll never become more effective or successful without it. Also, the person giving the feedback might someday be in a position to shape your future.

So, be *self-correcting*! Prove that you're listening and getting better every day (Appendix H).

Effective people thrive on feedback because their goal is to become more effective and successful.

16
BY
SETTING GOALS

"Setting goals is the first step in turning the invisible into the visible."
- Tony Robbins

Many people fall short because they fail to set their goals properly before trying to achieve them.

Stage 1: Setting the Goal

To set your goal that is both SMART and Personalized, you'll need a *Blueprint for Success*.

1. Is your goal SMART?

A SMART goal is:

S (Specific): Significant, Stretching, Simple.
M (Measurable): Meaningful, Motivational, Manageable.
A (Attainable): Achievable, Actionable, Aspirational.
R (Relevant): Results-oriented, Resourced, Realistic.
T (Timely): Time-specific, Timetabled, Time-limited.

Let's assume that your goal is:

To get a College Education.

Here are the questions to answer to create your SMART Goal Statement:

1. Is your Goal Attainable and Relevant?

To determine if your goal is attainable and relevant for you, it must pass these filtering questions:

- Is this goal my goal (or is it someone else's desire for me)?
- Is it okay for me to put my energy into this goal now?
- Can I fully commit myself emotionally to this goal?
- Can I visualize myself reaching this goal?

If you answered YES to all these questions, keep this goal on your list. Delete any goals where your answer was a NO, or I'm not sure.

2. Is your Goal Specific, Measurable, and Time-limited?

What specifically are you trying to accomplish? How do you know if you're getting closer to achieving your goal?

Goal: Get a College Education

This is what a SMART goal statement should eventually look like:

Goal: BS Degree in Engineering from ABC University (specific), no later than June 20XX (when – measurable and time-limited).

The no-later-than date above is your graduation date. What does your positive end-result look, sound, feel, smell, and taste like?

3. Is it Personal?

To make your goal personal, state your goal as a complete sentence in the 1st person, present tense: as if the goal has been completed.

Goal: I have my (1st person and present tense) BS Degree in Engineering from ABC University no later than June 20XX.

4. Is it Positive?

State your goals as a positive end-result using positive verbs like get, earn, or build. Avoid negative verbs like correct or avoid.

Goal: I have earned (positive verb) my BS Degree in Engineering from ABC University, no later than June 20XX.

5. Is it Inspiring?

Add positive emotional modifiers that inspire you.

Goal: I enjoy the confidence I feel (inspiring, positive emotion) by earning my BS Degree in Engineering from ABC no later than June 20XX.

You can now visualize a better life each time you attend class. Your motivation is directly linked to your emotions.

6. Is it Compelling?

Don't forget to add the compelling reason you're doing this.

Goal: I enjoy the confidence I feel by earning my BS Degree in Engineering from ABC no later than June 20XX, which I know will help me achieve my true career potential (the compelling reason).

17
BY
COMMITTING TO PURPOSE

*"I don't focus on what I'm up against.
I focus on my goals and I try to ignore the rest."
- Venus Williams*

A commitment is a duty, obligation, or responsibility, a promise or agreement to do something in the future, being bound emotionally or intellectually to a course of action or another person. It affects your effectiveness by how your treat your team members and how they work together.

Committing to purpose means mentally accepting your situation and making the best of it. Your purpose comes from letting go of your need to question, complain, or argue and to move toward total cooperation. You're *all in,* and there is no turning back because you've *burned-all-your-bridges.*

An excellent example is **Mother Teresa,** who never complained about having to work in the slums of Calcutta. She accepted her situation and did her best to ease the pain and suffering - one soul at a time. She was in an impossible situation that she knew she couldn't change. If you want committed team members, give them meaningful assignments, encouragement, support, and recognition. Commitment requires action. You can say you're committed, but the proof is in what you've done.

What if you run into obstacles?

You will run into obstacles along the way. Count on it. Some obstacles are known. Others are hidden and won't reveal themselves until the day before you finally achieve your goal.

The most dangerous obstacles lie between your ears.

Things will happen to throw you off course, like accidents, failure, illness, getting married, having children, or a death in the family. Now what? Pick up the pieces and keep going! Use these obstacles to strengthen you and drive you to greatness.

Never give up! Just find another way to get there.

What if you never reach your goal?

Follow this example. Pretend your goal was to achieve a net worth of $1 Million by the time you were 60, so you could comfortably retire. If, on your 60th birthday, your net worth was only $900,000, would you consider yourself a failure? You must be a failure if you don't reach your goal, right?

Here's the only important question to ask:

What would your net worth be today, without having the goal of $1 Million by age 60?

Without your goal, I'm confident in saying that your net worth would have been nowhere close to $900,000. Great job! Sometimes, getting close is good enough! Have faith!

How do you know if you're committed?

You know you've *committed to purpose* when you let go of all the negatives that have been holding you back, completely accept who you are and what you're doing, disengage from your struggles, no longer question or complain, forget about yourself, and resolve to fully cooperate without hesitation. When this happens, you've arrived; you've *committed to purpose*.

You can do this! Just take it one day at a time.

The next time you have Ham and Eggs for breakfast, stop to remember that the Chicken was involved, but the Pig was committed!

18
BY
OVERCOMING FEAR

"Danger is real, but fear is a choice."
- Will Smith, After Earth

What emotions have held you back all your life from doing, having, and being more than you are today? The day you were born, you came into this life with only two fears. What were they? Ask any pediatrician; the only fears babies have at birth are the *fear of loud noises* and the *fear of the dark*. All other fears are learned during your lifetime. Fears like speaking in public, jumping out of an airplane, snakes, spiders, and going to the dentist, you've learned.

Your fears often show up in the form of excuses, rationalizations, hesitation, indecision, and procrastination. Have you ever attempted to do something, but just as you went to start, you found yourself hesitating or stopping for some reason? This is called *resistance*, which we'll discuss later. Did you recognize what you were feeling?

The voice of Fear says...

> *"Yea, I know I need it, but it will; Take too long and will be too hard, Cost too much and took me away from my family. What if I fail?"*

At the root of most emotional roadblocks is some form of fear. Most of what you've feared over your entire lifetime never happened. It's perfectly all right to feel fear, to be afraid. In the face of real danger, if you're not afraid, you're either lying or mentally unbalanced. Fear is natural and normal. Fear (the fight or flight response) has been imprinted on your consciousness since the beginning of time. It's in your DNA through millions of years of evolution.

The greatest people of all time have confronted the same fears you face, but they acted despite their fears. They weren't immobilized. Sometimes fear can be a great *motivator and help keep you alive. A good example is hunting for a lion. Hunting for a lion is much more dangerous than deer hunting because the lion can kill you. Here, fear will help you do the right things to stay alive.

To learn more about *Awareness*, available at **Amazon.com**, see page 5.

The more you know about a situation, the quicker you can move through fear and achieve your goal. When there's no adverse consequence of acting, don't back away from the excitement of moving forward. All fear isn't false. You'll only know after you investigate it. Embrace it!

What are the most common types of fear?

The Fear of Failure:

I used to feel that there was such thing as failure. Failure only happens if you give up, but I was wrong!

True failure only happens if you suffer a loss.
The greater the loss – the greater the failure.

The only important question is, "What did you learn that can help you next time?" Failure can also be a great teacher, but only if you're paying attention. Paying attention means that you have identified the cause of the failure and have remembered the lesson for the next time.

Life has no rehearsals, only performances." – Anonymous.

Many people revisit their failures repeatedly because they forget the lesson. They forget what they learned from their past failures. If you don't learn the lessons the first time, you'll get a chance to do it all again. Failure is real and is often a great motivator. Don't run from your fears. Face them and embrace them. They'll follow you wherever you go unless you come to terms with them.

At the end of your life, you'll regret not having overcome your fears. So go after your dreams, no matter how big. Only then will you know your true potential. You have skills and abilities so vast that you couldn't begin to use them all in a hundred lifetimes. But, unfortunately, many people don't write their goals because they don't believe they're achievable.

Do you have the Freedom to FAIL?

> *"The greatest successes come from having the freedom to fail."*
> *- Mark Zuckerberg*

We all need room to make mistakes. The goal should be to learn from them and move forward without repeating them.

Here's an example:

The 2018 Volkswagen diesel engine debacle.

*According to many company executives, former CEO **Martin Winterkorn** was demanding, authoritarian, and abhorred failure. Unfortunately, he also fostered a climate of fear. The key to their aggressive growth was a new diesel engine that could lower emissions with higher efficiency. The problem was that the engine didn't meet the goals the CEO stated it would.*

The engineers were afraid to bring this failure to their boss and covered up the problem. When the truth was uncovered, it led to billions in losses and permanently damaged their brand.

Making honest mistakes is not a fire-able offense.
But failing to report a mistake could be.

Ask any successful person, and they'll tell you how failure and learning from it contributed to their success. Allowing members to make mistakes on their own, without the threat of immediate backlash from a boss or without blaming someone else, is one element to any member's growth.

Members need the freedom to make mistakes on the job to realize what needs to be done the next time to achieve the desired outcome.

Here's another good example:

"The 1953 graduating class from Yale was asked to write their goals before graduation. But, as you could imagine, most students ignored the request. Years later, at their 20th reunion, the 3% of the class that wrote down their goals before graduation compared notes to see how they had done. Much to their surprise, the 3% had accumulated a greater net worth than the remaining 97% of their classmates combined. Why? Because 97% were afraid to fail.

- 55 -

The Fear of Rejection (or the Fear of Asking).

The fear of someone saying NO is a powerful emotional roadblock to action until you realize that they're not rejecting you as a person, just your request. You may be asking the wrong person, the wrong question, or at the wrong time. This fear keeps you from asking for help from others. When in doubt, ask! Value yourself enough to get the answers needed to move forward.

The Fear of the Unknown:

The fear of dropping off the edge of the earth caused the entire human race to mistakenly believe the world was flat for thousands of years. Why? Because that's what their sense of sight told them. But, if you can't believe your senses, then what can you believe? How about the truth, for starters? And to obtain the truth, be willing to seek out and assess new information.

The Fear of Loss:

You'll work much harder to avoid a loss than to achieve a gain. So, use this knowledge to drive you to take action! The fear of loss is a powerful type of fear that is used against you every day.

If this is so powerful in getting people to act, can you use this as motivation to do things you don't want to do? Absolutely! The fear of loss can help you reach your goals.

For example, if you wanted to lose one pound per week, but you're having trouble staying true to your goal, try a little fear of loss and see what happens. If you gave me $1,000 in cash to hold for you with a written agreement that the money would belong to me if you failed to lose one pound per week for a month, and I'm doing the weighing, would that motivate you to lose weight? You bet! Because now you have something to lose, which will get your attention enough to take the actions needed to meet your goal.

The Fear of Success:

Fear of success is the fear that if you become rich and famous, you'll lose your old friends and must gain new ones. For some people, this thought is way outside their Comfort Zone. Also, if you've been told you would never amount to anything, how can you let those people down by proving them wrong?

The fear of success (the fear you'll lose your current friends or family) is a powerful force that keeps you as you are. If you expect more from life, you'll need the courage to attract new friends who have and do what you expect from your life. This doesn't mean that you'll have to abandon your current friends and family members. However, this will require stepping out of your Comfort Zone and acquiring new friends.

Throughout your life, you've held yourself back because of your fear - which wasn't real. Most of your fears in life are self-created because you willingly volunteered.

This page is intentionally left blank.

19
BY EXPANDING YOUR LEARNING ZONE

"The comfort zone is the great enemy to creativity; moving beyond it necessitates intuition, which in turn configures new perspectives and conquers fears."
- Dan Stevens

Do you know how to expand your learning zone to overcome the fear that has held you from achieving your true potential?

To better understand Fear, you must first understand your Comfort Zone. We all have a Comfort Zone, so that's no surprise. The surprise comes when you take a closer look at what really caused your Fear.

You might think that if you step outside your **Comfort Zone**, you'll be in your **Danger Zone**. After all, that's what you've learned over millions of years of evolution; it's called the *fight or flight response*.

There's great comfort in the familiar, simple, and predictable. We're all creatures of habit. But how do you gain experience if you stay in the familiar? How can you reach your true potential by staying in the familiar? Actually, you can't.

You'll never reach your true potential by staying in the familiar. You won't experience true joy by staying in your Comfort Zone.

Growth and excitement in life can only come from living outside your Comfort Zone, into the unknown, every second of your existence. But do you have to be in Danger to experience growth and excitement? No. You have three zones: your Comfort, Learning, and Danger Zone.

Your **Comfort Zone** is where you feel safe and warm. This is the zone you are in when watching TV and seeing other people skydiving, wishing it could be you.

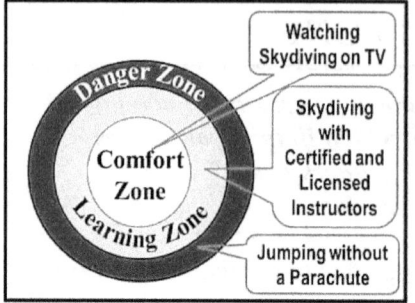

Next is your **Learning Zone**. This is the zone you are in when you're learning, growing, stretching, and achieving. This is the zone you are in when you are skydiving, with certified and licensed instructors. Yes, you were nervously excited and scared but glad to be alive.

And the last outer layer is your **Danger Zone**. This is the zone where your life is truly in danger. This is the zone you would be in if you jumped out of an airplane without a parachute.

Unfortunately, your brain's been hard-wired to believe that your Danger Zone and your Learning Zone are the same, and they're not! This means that most, if not all, of the Fear messages you've received during your lifetime, was when you were in your Learning Zone. Your brain still sends you danger messages when you're only trying to learn new things, trying new ways of doing things, striving to achieve your goals, stepping forward with new ideas, and meeting new people.

Your fears have stopped you from growing and living your life to its true potential – even though you were in no real danger.

I did dramatize this to show that being out of your Comfort Zone and into your Learning Zone is good for you. If you lived your life in your Learning Zone, every second of your existence, what an incredible life you'd have. Your Learning Zone is where you are when you are excited, growing, learning, achieving, reaching, stretching, struggling, and becoming better in the process. Being in your Learning Zone will also ensure you have nothing left to cross off from your "Bucket List" on your last day.

Life begins where your Comfort Zone ends.

20
BY DEMONSTRATING COURAGE

*"Courage is doing what you are afraid to do.
There can be no courage unless you are scared."
- Eddie Rickenbacker*

What types of courage are needed to become effective?

Physical courage is facing danger and acting despite it.

Moral courage is standing up for the truth, for what's right, for yourself, and for all those for whom you're responsible, even when you're the only one standing.

The fear of rejection or asking for a sale is difficult for most people. The fear of someone saying NO is a powerful emotional roadblock until you realize that they're not rejecting you as a person, just your request.

You may be asking the wrong person or asking the wrong question at the wrong time. This fear keeps you from asking for help from others. When in doubt, ask! Value yourself enough to get the answers you need to move forward.

Asking for help is a sign of strength, not a sign of weakness.

Not knowing you need help is a sign of ignorance.

Needing help and not asking for it is a sign of stupidity.

You can't control how others respond to you. However, you can control what you say and how you say it. Not everyone's going to say YES. Every NO isn't a personal rejection. An answer of NO is only a response to your presentation. It's also an indication of where the other person is coming from at the time you asked.

If you fail to go after what you want, you'll never have it.

If you're too afraid to ask, the answer will always be NO.

If you don't step forward, you'll always be where you are now.

Maybe the other person needs to be more informed to reach a YES. Also, since asking is a numbers game, every No response moves you closer to a YES, especially if you find out their reasons for saying NO.

Don't process an objection as a rejection.

Objections are usually a request for more information.

You have yet to give them a compelling enough reason to say YES. This is precisely why the best salespeople at the top of their profession finally close the sale (get a YES) only after receiving their fifth NO.

Asking is a numbers game – just ask anyone in sales.

They'll tell you that,

"Some will, Some won't, So what, Next."

Keep going! Don't let rejection stop you!

Assess why people repeatedly say NO and modify your future presentations accordingly. Re-educate them as to the real value of your request. You have no control over other people, places, things, and situations. However, you do control your thoughts, words, and deeds.

Tip:

> At the end of your interview for a position you really want, ask this question:

Do you have any concerns about my ability to fill this position?

> Regardless of their concerns, don't walk away. Stand your ground and add additional information and stories to make their concerns go away.

21
BY MAKING A PRESENTATION

"Being able to present or speak in public is one of five key business skills that can make or break your company or your career."
- Forbes Magazine.

What are the four most important phases to any presentation?

Phase 1
The Planning Phase

Step 1. The Purpose.

Why are you making this presentation? Your purpose should answer these questions. What message do you want them to take away? How will your message enhance their Happiness, Success, or Freedom?

Step 2. The Audience.

Who will be in the audience? Why are they attending? Find out what's important to them and tailor your presentation to your audience.

Step 3. The Location.

How many people will be attending, and is the location big enough? What type of visual aid works best in this location? Will everyone be able to see your visuals? Will you need to use a microphone?

Step 4. The Time.

How much time do you have? Should time be allocated at the end for questions? If your presentation is longer than 90-minutes, you'll need to give your audience at least a 15-minute break.

Phase 2
The Preparation Phase

Step 5. The Script.

Any good presentation script will include these three parts, The Opening, the Message, and the Closing.

Part 1. The Opening.

The most powerful parts of any good presentation should be your opening and closing. Your opening should include a welcome, an introduction, a purpose, and a brief outline of your talk. In addition, many speakers like to ask a rhetorical question to set the tone and have their audience ponder the answer.

Part 2. The Message.

The Main Points. The best presentations I've ever attended had no more than three main points that supported their message. Your talk should create a logical flow from your script to your visuals to queue you for what to say next.

Consider Humor. Stay away from humor involving sex, race, politics, or religion. Also, avoid humor about gender, politics, or sports. Humor involving children is a better choice. Also, animals are funny as well. But the best humor is when you make fun of yourself.

Audience Interaction. Some speakers like to be more interactive with their audience by asking questions during their talk. But what happens when you ask a question, and all you get is silence. When this happens, just pause and wait for a response. You don't have to keep talking to fill the silence. Silence is good. It means they're thinking.

Use Stories. We all love stories. They can be from your life, from someone else's life, or just imaginary stories.

> *However, the most powerful story I ever heard came from a speaker who told a powerful true story about a man named Bob. It was an amazing story about all Bob had sacrificed, overcame, and ultimately achieved. And just when I thought I couldn't be more amazed, the speaker revealed that he was Bob. The speaker had been telling his story all along. I was blown away.*

Part 3. The Closing.

Your closing should include a summary of your key points, your restated purpose (how your message will enhance their success, happiness, or freedom), and a Thank you! And I always like to end by asking, *what are your questions*

Step 6. The Editing.

Don't forget to edit your script by using *Grammarly.com* and the *2-Person Rule*. The *2-Person Rule* states that anything you write must be reviewed by a second person, someone on your team before the document goes out. The purpose of this rule is to make sure the communication makes sense (clear and understandable), doesn't leave anything out, is appropriate for the audience, is correct and error-free, and includes or excludes the right people.

Step 7. The Visuals.

The term visual here means anything you use to help keep you on-message. Before creating your visuals, take the time to visit *YouTube* and review both *"Slide Deck"* and *"Pitch Deck."* Those tired old PowerPoint bullet points from the past have been replaced by vivid color graphics with a few simple words like this:

From your script, create a draft of each visual to match your script. Remember, less is better! So, don't print every word from your script. Just use simple images with phrases to prompt you to talk about your next topic. Again, your visuals are not for your audience - they're for you. Your visuals should create a logical flow from your script to queue you to talk about next.

Step 8. The Backup Visuals.

And whenever I make a presentation, I always have a backup plan for my visuals, just in case something goes wrong. My backup is a simple paper handout showing all my visuals. The beauty of my handout is that now everyone can see my visuals, has the same information, has something to take notes on, and has something to take with them that has my contact information for future reference.

Step 9. The Microphone.

If you need a microphone, always use a lapel or a headset mike so your hands are free to gesture and you're free to move around. A podium mike chains you to the podium. And a hand-held mike takes away your ability to use both hands.

Step 10. Other Tasks.

As the presenter, your job is to present. Ask someone else to record attendance and take notes about what happened, the audience's reaction, and what questions were asked. Also, ask someone to help you keep track of time. Have them sit in the front row, and at the appropriate time, to show you two cards, one that says 5, meaning 5-MINUTES LEFT, and one that says STOP, meaning your times up.

Step 11. Read Ahead Materials.

A *Read Ahead Packet* is a collection of documents that attendees need to review before attending the presentation. This is intended to save time, generate conversation, and identify concerns or questions. If this is needed, get your packet out a week in advance.

Step 12. The Rehearsal and Practice.

This step is critical to your success (Chapter 30). Rehearse in the location, and with the mike and visuals, you'll have for your actual presentation. Have your team members ask you the questions you most anticipate receiving and candidly review your presentation.

Also, ask a team member to sit in the back of the room to see if they can hear you and see your visuals. The goal here is to minimize surprises and catch all your mistakes. Also, videotape yourself and review the video with others to correct any mistakes.

Phase 3
The Execution Phase

Step 1. Emotions.

It's completely normal to be nervous. The trick is not to let it show. The key is your breathing. Don't be afraid to pause and take a deep breath before continuing.

Step 2. Visual Aids.

Know your material so well that all you need to do is glance at your next visual to know what to say.

Step 3. Avoid these Common Mistakes.

Here are the most common mistakes presenters make:

- They talk to their visuals instead of their audience.
- They stand in front of and block their visuals.
- Their visuals are too small and too far away for anyone to see or read.
- They have way too much information jammed into one visual.
- They have too many people in too small a space. People in the back can't see the visuals or hear the speaker.

Step 4. Answer Questions.

When it comes to answering questions from the audience, this is what most new speakers dread the most. However, here are a few simple techniques.

- First, you can ask the audience to hold their questions until the end of your presentation. Or you could answer a question on the spot. However, doing so adds more time to your presentation.
- Second, you could say that their question will be answered later in the presentation.
- Third, if you're asked a question you can't answer, don't get flustered. Be honest and say that you don't know for sure, but if they'd leave their name and contact information, you'll get back to them in 48 hours.

Step 5. Maximize your Body Language.

When you speak, 55% of your message is communicated by your body language. And here are the most important components of your body language.

Facial Expressions. Your ability to smile and laugh will light up your presentation and makes you look more authentic and confident.

Eye Contact. Maintain strong eye contact with your audience or the senior person you're briefing.

Posture. The best speakers appear more relaxed by standing on one leg at a time and holding their hands naturally in front of them.

Movement. I recommend moving away from the podium and off the stage, so you're on the same level as your audience. You can move from side to side but always face your audience with good eye contact.

Hand Gestures. Your hands should be animated but always return to one central place in front of your body.

Step 6. Maximize your Voice.

When you speak, 38% of your message comes from your voice. Here are the most important components of your voice.

Tonality. Tonality is the most influential element of human communication. The tone of your voice is what gives meaning, both conscious and unconscious, to the message you're trying to send. It's not what you say, but how you say it, that creates an impression on everyone that hears you.

Tempo. The Tempo of your voice is the rate at which you speak. Speak slowly and distinctly. Don't be in such a big hurry. Also, pauses are powerful! Pauses add emphasis and cause your audience to pay more attention-anticipating what you'll say next. For a great example of how to use the power of the pause, watch this video on *YouTube, "Barack Obama's eulogy for Rep. **John Lewis**."*

Pitch. The Pitch of your voice is the degree of highness or lowness of your voice. Vary your Pitch from time to time to add emphasis and meaning to your presentation.

Volume. The volume of your voice is how loud or soft your voice is, which gives you the ability to project your voice. Vary the volume to add more emphasis and meaning.

Always have a water bottle close because your mouth will get dry, and don't be afraid to take a drink.

And in the end, I always like to ask, *"What are your questions?"* But then, if there are no more questions or my time is up, I always tell folks that I'll hang around after those who have further questions.

Phase 4
The Assessment Phase

After any presentation, here are the three most important steps.

Step 1. Conduct an After-Action Review.

After your presentation, sit down with your team and have an *After-Action Review* by answering these questions. Did everything go as rehearsed? Were there any surprises? What did we learn to make our next presentation even better?

Step 2. Prepare a Memorandum For Record.

After your *After-Action Review*, with the help of your team, create a memorandum for record documenting who was present and absent, what happened during the presentation, and any lessons learned. It's important that your boss and all team members receive a copy.

Step 3. Follow-through.

Your memo should clearly state what follow-through action is required. Keep track of it! Ensure everything that needs to be done gets done.

Success Tip:
Join Toastmasters.

If you'd like to raise the bar on your presentation skills, do yourself a favor; join Toastmasters International at Toastmasters.org. Your ability to make good presentations will dramatically enhance your career. Don't let your fear or pride get in your way. Seek out opportunities to present because that's the only way you'll ever get better.

This page is intentionally left blank.

22
BY BUILDING EFFECTIVE TEAMS

"A team is a small number of people with complementary skills who are committed to a common purpose, set of performance goals, and approach for which they hold themselves mutually accountable."
- The Leadership Edge

Effective people know that effective teams are the building blocks of greatness.

What do teams need to be effective?

- Strong leadership and common goals.
- Rules of the game (things they must do and must not do).
- A *Plan of Action* (POA) and support for risk-taking.
- 100% involvement and inclusion (access to information).
- Empowerment to overcome obstacles and distractions.
- To be held accountable for their results.

Team Building is a process of clarifying goals, building ownership across the team, and identifying obstacles and risk and removing or mitigating them.

If the risk can't be overcome, how can their effects be mitigated?

Can your team easily answer these questions?

- What's the team's purpose, and why is it important?
- Whom do they serve?
- What're the key things they deliver?
- What happens if they can't deliver these things?
- What does a "Win" look like for the team?

Teams, both in the field and in the office, are the building blocks of greatness.

Create a conversation between your team and your #1 customer to gain commitment, clarity, and alignment.

How do effective teams function?

The purpose of assembling a team is to accomplish bigger goals than any possible for members working alone. Therefore, effective bosses gather members and mold them into productive and effective teams.

Here are the most important behaviors of effective teams:

- **Commitment:** Only those committed to excellence are hired. New team members are selected by the team based on their levels of hard and soft skills.
- **Communications:** Members practice open and honest communications. They make a real effort to understand each other's points of view.
- **Contributions:** They contribute to success by applying their unique talents and knowledge to team assignments.
- **Cooperation:** Each member recognizes that conflict is a normal part of doing business. They view these situations as an opportunity for new ideas and creativity. They work to resolve conflict quickly and constructively.
- **Development:** They're encouraged to continually learn new skills and apply what they've learned on the job. They believe they have the support of the team.
- **Decision-making:** All participate in decisions affecting the team. But they understand the boss makes the final decision. Positive win/win, collaborative results are the goal always. Once the decision is made, they set aside their personal opinions and get to work executing the decision.
- **Interdependence:** Members recognize their interdependence and understand that personal and team goals are best accomplished with mutual support. Time isn't wasted over turf issues or attempts for personal gain at the expense of others.
- **Ownership:** They all feel a sense of ownership because they're committed to values-based common goals, which they create.
- **Structure:** Members work in a structured environment. They know what boundaries exist and who has final authority. The boss sets agreed-upon high standards of performance and is respected via active, willing participation.
- **Trust:** All members work in a climate of trust and are encouraged to openly express ideas, opinions, disagreements, and feelings. Questions are welcomed.

23
BY
BUILDING TRUST

"Better to trust the man who is frequently in error than the one who is never in doubt."
- Eric Sevareid

Trust is the glue that holds everything together for any company. Trust is important in business because it forms the basis of all relationships and interactions.

Trust is the firm belief in the reliability, honesty, integrity, ability, or strength of someone.

Creating a sense of trust is the most important factor when considering team member performance. Successful businesses are built on relationships, and the foundation of all relationships is trust. Unfortunately, there may be times when some people may not see eye to eye.

However, if members treat each other with respect and kindness and can get their ideas across without feeling belittled or discriminated against, then trust can be built. Without trust, your ability to come to an agreement or build consensus will always be compromised.

What are the benefits of trust?

- Increases productivity and improves morale.
- Enables members to work more effectively as a team.
- Reduces the time needed to discuss key issues and make *decisions.
- Facilitates cooperation and collaborative problem-solving.
- Improves effectiveness and diminishes costs.
- Expands teamwork and sustainability.

Trust is the emotional component of companionship, friendship, love, agreement, relaxation, and comfort.

*To learn more about *Decision-Making*, available at **Amazon.com**, see page 5.

Why are some bosses reluctant to delegate?

The main phobia bosses have about delegating is losing control. I get it. However, the truth is that you never had control in the first place.

Control over other people is an illusion!
But, influence, through persuasion, is achievable.

The sooner you realize this fact, the quicker you'll achieve order from chaos and let others do their job. The key to delegating is to do so gradually until you know who can move the work forward and who can't.

Are there different degrees of trust?

Here's a list showing the different degrees of trust, starting with showing *very little trust* and ending with showing *complete trust*:

- Bring the facts to me for action (little trust).
- Develop alternatives, and I'll take action based on the facts.
- Be prepared to take action, but don't do anything until I say so.
- Tell me what you propose to do and when.
- Analyze the situation, take action, and tell me the results.
- Just go! Here's the situation; deal with it! (complete trust).

How do you build trust?

Do you know the most important components of building relationships? You shouldn't be surprised that it's trust. How much does your boss trust you? How much trust do you have in your team members?

Here are the important components of building trust:

- If others sense that you're AUTHENTIC, you're much more likely to be trusted.
- If others sense that your LOGIC is solid, you're far more likely to be trusted.
- If others sense your EMPATHY is sincere and directed at them, you're far more likely to be trusted.

When all three are present, you have their trust. But if any one of these three is missing or needs work, trust is in question.

How can you become more Authentic?

In human relations, your lack of authenticity is considered bad faith in dealing with other people. You'll tend to hold back who you really are for fear that someone might dislike you.

Authenticity is the degree to which your actions congruent with your beliefs and desires, despite external pressures to conform.

You may even go so far as to be more like those with whom you work, hoping to fit in. Unfortunately, all this only makes you less likely to be trusted.

Pay less attention to what other people think about you and more attention to what you think about yourself. We all have an obligation to set and maintain the conditions that not only make it safe to be authentic but make it welcome. It's the key to achieving greater effectiveness.

How do you do it? You do it by being yourself and treating everyone with respect and kindness.

How can you use Logic?

Logic is the study of correct reasoning, especially as it involves the drawing of inferences.

Logic has two gates that you must pass through to be acceptable.

- It must be rational, reasonable, and doable.
- It must be *communicated in a manner that's easily understood, straightforward, and supported with evidence.

*To learn more about *Communicating*, available at **Amazon.com,** see page 5.

How can you show Empathy?

Empathy is the capacity to feel what another person is experiencing and place oneself in another's position.

There are two levels of empathy: Cognitive and Affective.

- **Cognitive empathy** means that you're capable of understanding other people's thoughts and feelings.
- **Affective empathy,** in addition to understanding, means that you're capable of feeling other people's emotions and of sharing their grief, suffering, and joy.

In addition to creating trust, these three skills can help you build an emotional connection with others and truly relate to their feelings. Empathy can be learned to help bring you closer to having greater success in your relationships.

Are you a Micro-Manager?

Well, let's see. The opposite of effective delegation is micromanagement, where a manager gives too much input, direction, and review.

Micromanagement is a management style whereby the boss closely observes and controls the work of a Direct Report.

Micromanagement also includes the suppression of constructive criticism leads to job turnover. In micromanagement, the boss not only tells the Direct Report WHAT to do but dictates HOW to do it. A frequent cause of micromanagement comes from the boss's doubt whether the Direct Report is competent enough to complete the project. Effective delegation requires a well-defined objective, a clear vision of the constraints and dependencies, and effective oversight.

So, are you a micro-manager? Do you trust your Direct Reports? Would they agree? Any room for improvement?

24
BY BUILDING CONSENSUS WITH A TEAM

"Unity is strength... when there is teamwork and collaboration, wonderful things can be achieved."
- Mattie Stepanek

Do you know how to achieve agreement from all team members that they can support a proposal? Few people in the workforce today understand the meaning and value of collaborating to build consensus.

The process of building consensus starts with collaboration.

Collaboration is the process of working with others to resolve a problem or achieve a goal.

Building consensus results from collaboration. Most people think that consensus means that everyone must like the proposal, the majority rules, or some other lame criteria - all of which are false.

Here's the truth!

Consensus is the desired end-product of collaboration intended to achieve agreement from all team members that they can support a proposal.

Support means that each member agrees that the proposal will work and commits to doing all they can to ensure its success.

If not, this is their chance to speak up! The process of building consensus gives every member the freedom to voice their agreements or disagreements before consensus is achieved. It's also intended to be inclusive, participatory, and cooperative, seeking opinions and input from all members.

Consensus uses common agreement to resolve mutually exclusive positions. It's not the majority rules, nor a popularity contest. It doesn't care whose proposal is being considered or if any member likes or dislikes the proposal. It only asks each member if they can support the proposal. If not, a valid reason must be provided.

VALID means that their reason must be either a better proposal or a fact and not an opinion.

Why is building consensus important?

To answer this question, I always ask,

What's the Greatest Hunger of the Human Heart?

What does every human being need to be fulfilled at work?

The Greatest Hunger of the Human Heart is to be NEEDED.

To be needed means:

- To be seen means to be included and validated.
- To be heard means to be listened to, understood, and appreciated.
- To be valued means to be recognized for their contributions.
- To be treated with respect and kindness because they matter.

The greatest hunger of the human heart is to be seen, heard, valued, and treated with respect and kindness because they matter.

If team members aren't allowed to *"speak their piece,"* you're telling them that they're not important and they don't matter. Not good! Do you feel needed where you work? Do those who work with you feel needed? Do you treat everyone with respect and kindness-no matter what?

Everyone needs to be engaged, involved, and have a say concerning the things that affect their wellbeing.

This is why consensus building is so powerful.

When's consensus needed?

Consensus is needed whenever you're trying to resolve a problem, create a plan, or make any change that affects the team.

What are the benefits of building consensus?

- Consensus building improves the proposal by using the wisdom and knowledge of the team.
- It uncovers any Unintended Consequences and Second and Third-Order Effects that could slow or stop the proposal.
- It builds trust and commitment from the team by engaging them and using their input.

Building consensus is far more important than achieving it because, in the end, everyone may not agree to support the proposal, but at least they've been included in the process.

Failure to build consensus will erode teamwork, commitment and cause the failure to consistently produce excellent results. Building consensus sounds easy, but it's not. However, it's worth it because, without their involvement, they'll never be committed! And without their commitment, you'll never be able to consistently produce excellent results!

By building Consensus

Here are two methods of building consensus:

- **Staffing a Proposal.** This means circulating a proposal document through all team members to obtain their concurrence or non-concurrence with comments.
- **Conducting a Team Meeting.** This method works best when the proposal is an important decision that's time-sensitive, involves major funding, and affects the entire team.

If this is the case, here are the most important steps to build consensus.

Step 1. Discuss the proposal.

Gather the team, either at one location or on a phone or video conference, and discuss the proposal.

- **If the proposal is a problem,** how was it discovered, how bad is it, and what're the risks if it continues unresolved? What's causing this problem? Is this the real problem or just a symptom? And how do we know for sure?
- **If the proposal is a goal,** why is it important? What's the intended benefit?

Step 2. Discuss the Solution.

If the solution is obvious, then work with the team to create the *Plan of Action* to implement the solution. If there could be several solutions, conduct a *Brainstorming Session* and select the best solution (Chapter 21).

Step 3. Anticipate the Consequences and Effects.

Once the solution has been identified, discuss the possible *Unintended Consequences* and *Second and Third-Order Effects* (Chapter 11).

Step 4. Eliminate all Unresolved Issues.

Discuss and identify all *Unresolved Issues* (any question, unknown, concern, shortfall, obstacle, or problem) that could slow or stop your progress (Chapter 10).

Step 5. Ask for Consensus.

Now, ask all team members if they can support the proposal. If not, why? Remember,

Support means that each member agrees that the proposal will work and commits to doing all they can to ensure its success.

If all members agree, ask them to create the *Plan of Action* to implement the proposed solution. If any member has a valid reason for non-support, continue to Step 6.

By resolving Reasons for Non-Support

At this point, only valid reasons should be considered. However, real-life doesn't work that way. Members will always have concerns and opinions, and they need to be heard. Here are the most important steps.

Step 6. Deal with their concerns.

If a member has a concern or opinion that's not a fact, this is when things get interesting.

- If their concern is that it's **too costly**, what does he mean? Too costly compared to what? How can the cost be reduced or offset? What's the contingency plan if it does cost more?
- If their concern is that it **will take much longer**, what's he basing this on? What's the downside if it does take longer? What's our Contingency Plan if it does?
- If their concern is that it's **too risky**, what does he mean? Can it be mitigated? Can a contingency plan be created just in case?

Step 7. Convert Reasons to Risks.

Before continuing, exchange the term *"Reason"* for *"Risk."* This will make this process much easier to understand. And for each risk, there are two critical things you must consider, probability and impact.

Step 8. What's the Probability?

How likely is this risk to happen (Chapter 12)? If the probability is *Low*, place the risk, *On-Hold*. This means that it's been noted and set aside temporarily. If the probability is *Medium* to *High*, or you're unsure, continue to the next step.

Step 9. What's the Impact?

What's the Impact or Effect on the proposal when this risk happens (Chapter 12)? If the Impact is *Minor,* place the risk *On-Hold*. If the Impact is *Moderate* to *Significant*, or you're unsure, continue to Step 10.

Step 10. Can the Risk be Mitigated?

- If the risk can be mitigated, create a *Contingency Plan* (Chapter 15).
- If the risk can't be mitigated, you still have three options (Chapter 14).

Remember, you don't need a consensus before sending the proposal to your boss for approval. However, you'll need to include all reasons for non-support and let your boss decide. All members don't have to like the solution! They just need to be able to support it.

By Staffing a Proposal

Here's another method of building consensus without a meeting.

Staffing is the process of circulating a proposal document to all team members to obtain their concurrence or non-concurrence with comments in writing.

This method works best in situations where the proposal is routine and not time-sensitive. The proposal document could be a procedure, plan, question, or idea. Here are the four most important steps.

Step 1. Provide the proposal document to all members.

Ensure each team member receives a copy of the proposal document. Ask each member for their concurrence or non-concurrence with comments. And don't forget to provide a deadline.

Step 2. Resolve non-concur comments.

When member comments are returned to you, you may need to visit some members privately to better understand their comments and determine if adjusting your proposal could lead to their concurrence. Remember, concurrence means that each member agrees that:

The proposal will work and commits to doing all they can to ensure its success.

If not, a valid reason must be provided, which means their non-concur comments must be a better proposal or a fact and not an opinion.

Step 3. Make changes.

If you need to make changes, you'll need to send the revised proposal to all members again for another review. And for the second review, ensure you highlight any changes made from the first review.

Step 4. Obtain approval.

Note: You don't need the concurrence of all team members before sending your proposal to your boss for approval, but you'll need their reasons for non-concurrence. Remember, building consensus should never be done in a vacuum. You need the feedback to help you see beyond your blind spots.

25
BY COACHING FOR PEAK PERFORMANCE

"Failure is good. It's fertilizer. Everything I've learned about coaching, I've learned from making mistakes."
- Rick Pitino

Do you know how to coach others to achieve *Peak Performance?*

Coaching is your ability to facilitate, guide, and be a strategic resource to support a member's progress towards his self-determined objectives by demonstrating perceptiveness, integrity, and truth-telling.

Effective people know that coaching is a results-oriented, quality-focused process and a *cutting-edge* system to improve personal and team effectiveness.

Ask more, Tell less!

The coach facilitates the member's growth through a series of *Socratic* questioning (deductive) and doesn't profess to have all the answers. However, mutual accountability and trust and the depth of the coach's experience give the process its power and effectiveness.

Here are the three most important features that make coaching work.

> **Synergy:** Here, the member and the Coach become a team by focusing on the member's goals and needs and accomplishing more than the member would alone.
>
> **Structure:** With a Coach, a member takes more actions, thinks bigger, and gets the job done due to the accountability the Coach encourages
>
> **Expertise:** The Coach has some knowledge or experiences the member needs.

What's the Coach's Job?

>   Help the member establish written goals.
>
>   Turn breakdowns into breakthroughs.
>
>   Encourage accountability.

Teach or mentor.

Help the member make a quantum leap.

What's the Team Member's Job?

Tell the truth.

Be prepared.

Stay in action.

Be on time for conversations.

Be accountable.

Coaching is a system centered on listening, asking, leading, and honoring. Coaching is not telling or supervising. It's different. Coaching doesn't encourage co-dependency, lack of accountability, or making excuses. It encourages just the opposite.

What Tools does a Coach use?

Listening: So, the member feels heard and supported.

Asking questions: So, the member uncovers his answers.

Requesting actions: So, the member stays on-track.

Intuiting: So, the truth is revealed.

What Format does a Coach use?

Member and coach agree upon an exciting goal.

Member visits coach to check progress.

Conversations are limited to no more than one hour

Both have an agenda for each conversation.

Member tracks results for reporting to the Coach.

What does the Coach ask during each session?

What was your intended goal?

How far along should you be by today?

Where are you?

What were your obstacles?

What were your accomplishments?

What's your plan going forward?

What're you keeping a secret and not telling me?

What Techniques does a Coach Use?

Coaching is a wonderful skill. The coaching skill I'm referring to is asking better questions and having the member come to his conclusions and solutions. The easiest way to explain coaching techniques is to use the example of **Dr. Phil McGraw**. He uses reality therapy along with the *Insanity Test, the Truth Test, and the Take-away.*

The Insanity Test:

Have you ever been guilty of insane behavior? We all have on many occasions.

Insane behavior is doing the same thing over and over again while expecting a different result.

The Truth Test:

The *Truth Test* is when *Dr. Phil* asks his clients,

"How's that workin out for ya?"

If what you've been doing is not producing the results you're seeking, then why are you still doing the same old thing? Why not try something new?

"What do you need to do?"

These questions help the member come to his conclusions. This process is desirable because the member is the one who must execute the solution. If he came up with the solution on his own, he'd be much more likely to take ownership of the solution.

This is coaching at its best, asking better questions and letting the member decide what needs to be done. If they have no clue what to do, offer suggestions, but let them decide what needs to be done.

Then, get them to commit to a *Plan of Action* over a specified period and reassess the results. Then, adjust from there. When you tell someone what to do, that's consulting or advising, but certainly not coaching.

The Take-Away:

This is a powerful technique and uses the withdrawal of something, which taps into their innate *fear of loss* and sounds something like this:

> *"This is probably not right for you."*
>
> *"You probably wouldn't qualify."*

"The timing for you to do this is probably not the best right now."

> *"I don't think this is going to work for you."*

It normally generates a response like, "What do you mean? What's wrong with me? Why wouldn't I qualify?"

Now, you've got their attention because no one wants to lose anything – even if they don't have it yet. Now they want it more. Make sense? In this case, the Coach could withdraw his coaching.

26
BY MANAGING RISK

There is only one big risk you should avoid at all costs, and that is the risk of doing nothing."
- Denis Waitley

Effective people understand the effects of risk in the workplace and how critical it is to their probability of success.

Simply Stated, RISK is Uncertainty!

Managing anything requires the ability to anticipate and mitigate risk. You can't control everything that happens to you, but you can control your degree of preparation and how you respond.

Here are the most important things to consider when assessing risk:

1. Reduce the Risk of Failure.

By planning for risk to occur, you're decreasing your probability of failure, which increases your probability of success. Much of this is done every day in your organizations. It's called risk reduction, like having fire, theft, and liability insurance (Chapter 28).

2. Understand that control is an illusion.

This simple prayer, which I learned during my recovery from alcoholism, helped me finally answer this life-altering question:

What are the only things in life I can control and therefore change?

THE SERENITY PRAYER

"God, grant me the Serenity to
Accept the things I cannot change,
Courage to change the things I can,
and the Wisdom to know the difference
- Reinhold Niebuhr

And these answers changed my life forever.

**In this life,
You cannot control or change other people,
places, things, situations, or circumstances.**

**The only things you can control and therefore
change are your thoughts, words, and deeds.**

And all those years, I thought I could control and change other people. What a waste of time and energy. This may come as a shocking epiphany for many of you because you've probably made the same mistake.

Yes, you can influence them, but you can't control or change them. You can only control and therefore change yourself.

This concept is crucial because until you learn to truly control what you can control (your thoughts, words, and deeds), you'll never influence anyone to help you consistently produce excellent results.

3. Identify your Risk Goals.

When it comes to managing risk, you should always have two goals.

- Make the **Risk** LESS likely to happen, like putting training wheels on your child's bicycle.

- Make the **Impact** LESS severe when, and NOT if it happens, like requiring your child to wear a safety helmet.

4. Plan for both Anticipated and Unanticipated Risk.

In life, there are always two categories of risk:

- *Anticipated Risks* are those risks that include all the things that could *reasonably-go-wrong*, including anything that could slow or stop your project or cause injury, illness, accident, death, security violations, property damage, or financial loss.

- *Unanticipated Risks* are those Risks that you could not possibly have predicted (Chapter 29).

5. Conduct a Risk Assessment.

With the help of your team, conduct a *Risk Assessment*.

Anticipated Risk comes in two forms:

- **Bad Internal Situations** are things that don't require a call to 911, like equipment breakdowns, people being late, cell phone batteries going dead, and other mistakes, defects, or errors.
- **Bad External Situations** are things that require a call to 911, like fire, injuries, accidents, property damage, violence, or theft.

6. Assess the Impact and Probability.

For each Bad Situation, assess these two critical things:

- **Impact** means how this Bad Situation will affect your project and is rated as *Significant, Moderate, or Minor*. Based on your assessment, when, and not if, this Bad Situation happens, how serious will it affect your project?
- **Probability** means how likely is this Bad Situation to happen and is rated as *High, Medium, or Low*. Based on your assessment, how likely is this Bad Situation to occur?

7. Assess your Risk Options.

Option 1. AVOID the Risk.

In some cases, you may want to avoid the risk altogether. This could mean not getting involved or just deleting a high-risk activity. This is a good option when taking the risk involves no advantage or when the cost of mitigating isn't worth the risk. However, when you avoid potential risks, you may miss an opportunity.

So, do your *What if Analysis* to explore your options before deciding. *What-if Analysis* is used to conduct advanced business analysis on different scenarios in Excel.

Option 2. SHARE the Risk!

You could decide to share the risk and the potential gain with others. For example, you share risks when you ensure your project site or partner with another organization.

Option 3. ACCEPT the Risk.

This option is usually best under these conditions:

- When there's nothing you can do to prevent the risk.
- When the potential loss is less than the cost of insuring against the risk.
- When the potential gain is worth accepting the risk.

For example, you might accept the risk of a project launching late if the potential sales will still cover your costs.

8. Beware of Scope Creep.

Scope means the size of the project and its requirements, complexity, and goals. Scope creep occurs when others want to make changes to your project. So, negotiate these changes to gain either more time or more money, or both.

9. Create Contingency Plans.

The purpose of a *Contingency Plan* (Chapter 29) is to diminish the severity of a Bad Situation. *Contingency Plans* need to be *Staffed* (Chapter 24) through all Key Players and approved by your boss.

10. Use Preventive Actions.

How do you find problems, or do you wait until they find you? *Preventive Actions* are all the things you should be doing 30, 60, or 90 days before any project to uncover all your Pre-Problems. Pre-Problems are mistakes, defects, shortfalls, omissions, errors, or anything else that could slow or stop your work. *Preventive Actions* should be added to your *Project's Timetable (Appendix B)*.

*To learn more about **Planning**, available at **Amazon.com,** see page 5.

27
BY CONDUCTING A RISK ASSESSMENT

"Take risks: if you win, you will be happy;
if you lose, you will be wise."
- Unknown

Effective people know that conducting a good *Risk Assessment* is critical to their probability of success. You can't control everything that happens to you, but you can control your degree of preparation and how you respond. With the help of your team, conduct a good *Risk Assessment* by *Brainstorming* (Chapter 31) anything related to your work that could *reasonably-go-wrong*.

Here are the most important steps to conduct a good *Risk Assessment*.

Step 1. Anticipate the Physical Risks.

Have you inspected the site for anything that could cause an injury, accident, illness, or death? How about safety, sanitation, and access for those with disabilities - any risk there?

Step 2. Anticipate the Security Risks.

- **For *cybersecurity*,** what could cause a data breach, loss of personal info or intellectual property, or a disruption of services?

- **For *physical security*,** what could permit unauthorized access leading to theft or property damage?

Step 3. Anticipate the Financial Risk.

- What could cause financial loss through fraud, waste, or abuse?
- What insurance is needed, and is it current?

Step 4. Anticipate the Operational Risks.

- What's the *Impact* when these risks occur (Chapter 26)?
- What's the *Probability* these risks will happen (Chapter 26)?
- How can these risks be mitigated (Chapter 28)?
- What's your *Contingency Plan* for when they do (Chapter 29)?

- Do your team members know how to take *Immediate Action* (Appendix F)?
- What assumptions are needed to move the work forward?
- What *Preventive Actions* did you add to your *Plan of Action (POA) Timetable* (Appendix B)?
- Have you *Staffed* your POA (Chapter 24) with the team, and what was the result?
- What are you forgetting to do (Appendix E)?

Step 5. Eliminate Unresolved Issues.

What are all the questions, unknowns, concerns, shortfalls, obstacles, or problems that could slow or stop our progress (Chapter 32)?

Step 6. Anticipate and Mitigate Unintended Consequences.

Unintended Consequences are the outcomes that aren't expected by your actions (Chapter 33).

Step 7. Anticipate Second and Third-Order Effects.

Second and Third-Order Effects focus on how your recommendations or decisions affect others at different levels in your organization (Chapter 33).

Step 8. Anticipate the Risk of Bad Situations.

- **Bad Internal Situations** are situations that *don't require a call to 911*, like equipment breakdowns, people being late, cell phone batteries going dead, mistakes, defects, or errors.
- **Bad External Situations** are situations that *require a call to 911*, like fire, injuries, accidents, property damage, violence, or theft (Chapter 28).

If you fail to conduct a good *Risk Assessment* before your next project, do so at your peril.

You've been WARNED!

28
BY MITIGATING THE RISK TO BAD SITUATIONS

"If you are not living on the edge, you are taking up too much room."
- Jayne Howard

To manage anything, you need to know how to mitigate your risk. In business, there are two different types of risk: Internal and External.

By mitigating the Risk to Bad Internal Situations

This includes equipment breakdowns, people being late, cell phone batteries going dead, and other mistakes, defects, or errors.

Bad Internal Situations are situations that don't require a call to 911.

Once you've determined everything that could *reasonably-go-wrong*, you're ready to mitigate the risks. Here are the most important steps.

Step 1. Brainstorm.

Conduct a *Brainstorming Session* to determine what actions are needed to respond to each bad situation (Appendix D).

Step 2. Create Contingency Plans.

Now that you've determined what actions are needed for each Bad Internal Situation, it's time to create a *CONPLAN* for each (Chapter 29).

Step 3. Rehearse each CONPLAN.

Rehearse each *CONPLAN* a few days before your project to identify any errors, omissions, or misunderstandings. Don't just ask people if they're ready. Ask them to show you that they're ready (Chapter 30).

Step 4. Eliminate All Unresolved Issues.

Continue to eliminate all *Unresolved Issues* by facilitating collaborative problem-solving to build consensus (Chapter 32).

By mitigating the Risk to Bad External Situations

The truth is that even though local first responders have more resources and training than you, you can still make the risk less likely to happen and make the impact less severe when it occurs.

Bad External Situations are those that require a call to 911.

Here are the most important steps to mitigate the risk of Bad External Situations.

Step 1. Assess the Risk of Fire.

Since most fires start as small fires, do you have more fire extinguishers on-site than you need? Do people know where they're located and how to use them? Have they been tested and inspected? Are there sufficient smoke detectors present and serviceable? Are there any local restrictions on burning, building fires, or fire warnings?

Step 2. Assess the Risk of Medical Issues.

Do you have first aid kits on-site, with staff trained on how to administer first aid? When were these kits last inspected and replenished? Can ambulances be located closer to your venue? Do you have staff trained to administer CPR? Do defibrillators be centrally located with staff trained in how to use them?

What about those who have food allergies and those allergic to bee stings? And how about mosquitos, the elderly, and the disabled? Are there any unsafe conditions that could lead to an injury or accident? Are there any unsanitary conditions that could lead to illness?

Step 3. Assess the Risk of Crime.

Whenever assessing the risk of crime, always consider:

- **Access control** means entry denial, metal detectors, gates, locks, keys, fences, barriers, checkpoints, firewalls, passwords, and badges.

- **Deterrence** means cameras, guards, dogs, signs, security lighting, punishment for violators, and barbed wire.

- **Early warning** means alarms, security systems, loudspeakers, intercom, flashing lights, police alerts, lockdowns, and sirens.

29
BY CREATING CONTINGENCY PLANS

"If you don't risk anything you risk even more."
- Erica Jong

Do you know how to create a plan to respond to anticipated bad situations?

Contingency Plans (or CONPLAN) are Plans of Action that assumes that an anticipated bad situation has occurred.

Have you ever been involved with a project when things went wrong? What did you do? Was there a *Contingency Plan,* and was it rehearsed? A *CONPLAN* is only executed when something bad happens. Being prepared is the key! What's your plan? Remember,

Many bad situations never become a problem because someone knew what to do and had the resources to respond.

Here are the most important steps.

Step 1. Collaborate.

Once you've identified all the bad things that could *reasonably-go-wrong,* collaborate with your team to determine what actions should be taken in response.

Step 2. Assess the Impact.

Impact means how this Bad Situation will affect your project and is rated as *Significant, Moderate, or Minor.* Based on your assessment, when, and not if, this Bad Situation happens, how serious will it affect your project?

Step 3. Assess the Probability.

Probability means how likely is this Bad Situation to happen and is rated as *High, Medium, or Low.* Based on your assessment, how likely is this Bad Situation to occur? If you have a bad situation with a Significant Impact and a High Probability of occurring, you'll need lots of help.

Step 4. Create a CONPLAN.

Once you've identified the actions that should be taken, create a CONPLAN to deal with each Bad Situation. Each CONPLAN uses the same format as a *Plan of Action* but begins with an assumption. This assumption is the Bad Situation that you and your team have already anticipated. Your CONPLAN tells the reader exactly what to do when the assumption becomes true. It also lists what's needed, where it's stored, and how to use it.

Let's assume that you were assigned as the Project Manager for your company's *Team Building Session* in Buffalo, NY, in January. You and your team have already anticipated three Bad Internal Situations that could *reasonably-go-wrong* with your project.

- **For guests arriving late,** you assessed the Impact to be *Significant* because the Team Building Session won't be effective without all guests. However, you assessed your probability to be *Medium* because of the weather in Buffalo this time of year. So, for guests arriving late, you intend to use CONPLAN A.

- **For transporting guests to the resort,** you assessed the Impact to be *Moderate* because of the weather, the fact that the resort is 27 miles away, and that delays will disrupt the success of the team building session. And you assessed the probability to be *Medium* because you know that the weather in Buffalo this time of year is always a challenge. So, for Transporting guests to the resort, you intend to use CONPLAN B.

- **For lost baggage,** you assessed the Impact to be *Minor* because your activity can still go on regardless. However, you assessed the Probability to be *High* because the airlines in the winter have a history of losing luggage. So, for lost baggage, you intend to use CONPLAN C.

Step 5. Create your Risk Matrix.

Here's an example of a *Risk Matrix*.

Risk Matrix for Team Building Session			
BAD SITUATION	IMPACT	PROBABILITY	CONPLAN
Guests Arriving Late	Significant (8-10)	Medium (4-7)	A
Transport to Resort	Moderate (4-7)	Medium (4-7)	B
Lost Baggage	Minor (1-3)	High (8-10)	C

Notice that this simple table shows all Bad Internal Situations, their Impact, Probability, and which CONPLAN to use.

Note: The risk numbers 1 through 10 above are used to help create your *Risk Threshold*.

Step 6. Assess your Risk Threshold.

Here's an example of a *Risk Threshold Table*.

Risk Threshold = Impact X Probability.		
Risk Rating	Risk Range	Remarks
CRITICAL	50 or higher	The acceptable risk threshold for safety and health should always be lower than your financial or operational risks.
MEDIUM	16 to 49	
LOW	15 or Lower	

Notice that this table shows that a *risk threshold*, rated from critical to medium to low, is the sum of the impact times the probability. Knowing your risk threshold is important because your acceptable safety and health risk threshold should always be lower than your financial or operational risks.

Ideally, you should be doing all you can to reduce your risk. And if you can't, you'll need a good CONPLAN ready to respond.

Step 7. Staff your CONPLANs.

Staff your CONPLANs through all Key Players for their concurrence or non-concurrence with comments (Chapter 24).

Step 8. Obtain Approval.

Present your CONPLANs to your boss for approval with all the comments from your Key Players attached.

Step 9. Distribute your CONPLANs.

Once approved, ensure that all Key Players have a copy of all CONPLANs well before the project starts.

Step 10. Rehearse your CONPLANs.

A few days before your project starts, rehearse your CONPLANs with all Key Players (Chapter 30).

30
BY CONDUCTING A REHEARSAL

"Take calculated risks. That is quite different from being rash."
- George S. Patton

Have you ever conducted or participated in a project where no one knew what was going on? How did that make you feel?

By Rehearsing

A Rehearsal is the process of reviewing (looking at) the results of others before they get in front of your boss to ensure all Pre-Problems (mistakes, defects, shortfalls, omissions, or errors) have been resolved.

The type of rehearsal I'm referring to here is to examine everything concerning your project BEFORE your boss sees it. How hard is that?

Why do you think weddings have rehearsals?

Do you have the ring, know where to stand, know what to say, and know the sequence of what's going to happen next? And why does it matter? Who wants it to be perfect? Enough said. What do you need to see, test, or practice a few days before your project starts?

Get a Clue! Even criminals have rehearsals because they know the consequences if they don't.

Rehearsals include things like previews, layouts, practice, a sand-table, or white-board walk-throughs. They also include demonstrations, role-playing, document reviews, and testing. And when your rehearsal uncovers a flaw, have it fixed and have another rehearsal.

Caution! Never ask people, *"are you ready?"* Instead, say, *"Show me that you're ready. I want to see it!"* What's stopping you?

> Look, I can't tell you how many times I've been burned by people who've said to me that they were ready when they weren't. So, do yourself a favor. If this is your project, your job is to check. That means looking at everything before it gets in front of your boss.

By Practicing

As a child, I was told that *"Practice makes perfect."* As an adult, I learned that this was false. It should be,

"Perfect practice makes perfect."

If you're practicing the wrong way, your results will suffer. That's why you always need a coach, someone who can show you how it should be done correctly to achieve the best result.

My favorite practice quote comes from **Coach Paul *"Bear"* Bryant**.

> *"It's not the will to win that matters – everyone has that. It's the will to prepare (or practice) to win that matters."*

It's no wonder Coach Bryant amassed six national championships and thirteen conference championships as the head coach of the University of Alabama's football team.

Growing up, I also learned that to be the best, I needed to *"Practice until I got it right."*

However, much later in life, I found that to master anything, I needed to

"Practice until I couldn't get it wrong."

The best example of this comes from **Mary Lou Retton,** who won the gold medal in the 1984 Olympics in LA. She scored a perfect 10 in the vault competition.

After that vault, she asked the judges if she could do it again to show it wasn't just a lucky vault. Her score was another perfect 10. More impressive was that she was a sophomore in high school, had recently had leg surgery, and won two silver medals and two bronze medals.

Her performance was historic because she was the first-ever American woman to win the all-around gold medal at the Olympics, making her the most popular athlete in the US.

31
BY CONDUCTING A BRAINSTORMING SESSION

"To win without risk is to triumph without glory."
- Pierre Corneille

How many times have you just assumed that you knew the BEST solution to a problem, only to find out later that you were wrong? Effective people know the value of *Brainstorming* when resolving problems and achieving goals (Chapter 31).

Brainstorming is a group process of producing the most potential options to resolve a problem or achieve a goal.

Here are the most important steps.

Step 1. Pick your team.

Keep your group small (seven or less). If more than seven members, break them into smaller groups and compare the results.

Step 2. Use Mindstorming (Optional!).

The day before, give each team member a sealed envelope with instructions not to open it until they get home that night. Inside the envelope are instructions to conduct a *Mindstorming Exercise* by writing down many potential solutions to a problem. Also, ask them not to share their options before the meeting the next day.

Step 3. Prepare needed materials.

You'll need a blackboard, whiteboard, or some large sheets of paper on a vertical easel, wide-tipped markers to record all options for all to see.

Step 4. Decide how you'll participate.

Some members may not feel comfortable if you conduct the session. If you ever feel that your presence could diminish the team's effectiveness, find something else to do.

Step 5. Assign other duties.

If needed, select someone else to facilitate the *Brainstorming Session* and assign another member to act as the *Scribe* to record each option.

Step 6. Conduct the meeting.

A good *Brainstorming Session* should consist of these three phases.

Phase I. Capture All Options:

Limit this phase to 10-15 minutes or just enough time for each member to present their options. In this phase, you're looking for volume only. Judgment or criticism is reserved for the next phase.

Phase II. Discuss all Options:

After capturing everyone's options, this phase is where discussion is encouraged and options are consolidated.

Phase III. Validate each Option by using the *"Common-Sense Test:"*

This phase is designed to assess the validity of each option by using the *Common-Sense Test*. This test asks five questions about each option to qualify it as a valid option. If any option receives a *"No"* or *"we're not sure"* answer, it's eliminated.

1. **Is it Suitable?** Does the option solve the problem, and is it legal and ethical?

2. **Is it Feasible?** Does it fit within available or easily acquirable resources?

3. **Is it Acceptable?** Is it worth the cost and the risk?

4. **Is it Distinguishable?** Does it differ significantly from other options?

5. **Is it Complete?** Does it solve the problem from start to finish?

Step 7. Select the Best.

In the end, you should have a list of valid options that require further research to help you select the best option. *Brainstorming* helps build commitment. Since you've included the team in the selection process, they'll be more committed when the time comes to implement the best option.

Involvement builds commitment, and commitment is critical to the consistent production of excellent results.

32
BY ELIMINATING UNRESOLVED ISSUES

> *"There are two ways of spreading light: to be the candle or the mirror that reflects it."*
> *- Edith Wharton*

Effective people know that eliminating all the *uncertainty* associated with their work will enhance their probability of success and improve their credibility with their boss.

> **An Unresolved Issue is any question, unknown, concern, shortfall, obstacle, or problem that could slow or stop your progress.**

This process directly seeks out and mitigates any risk that lies in your path. These hidden risks are called *"Uncertainty."*

Your mission is to hunt down and eliminate all the "Uncertainty" associated with your work.

If you don't, *Murphy's Law* will surely ruin your day. Don't let this happen to you!

So, do yourself a favor. Identify and eliminate all your *Unresolved Issues* early on to avoid the frustration, mistakes, and potential failure that could result from not having your act together.

Here are the most important steps to eliminate all your *Unresolved Issues*.

Step 1. Identify all Issues.

To identify all your *Unresolved Issues*, seek good answers to these questions.

- What do we need to know - but don't?
- What do we know for sure, but the answer is unsatisfactory or unacceptable?
- What are all things we need but don't have?

- What are all the questions, unknowns, concerns, shortfalls, obstacles, or problems that could slow or stop your progress?
- Who has done this type of work before, and what were their problems, consequences, and effects?
- What are we forgetting to do (Appendix E)?

Step 2. State each issue in one sentence.

Each *Unresolved Issue* should be stated in one sentence and answer these questions.

- What do we need specifically?
- How much (or how many) do we need, exactly?
- Why do we need it - the purpose?
- When's the latest we need it?
- Where do we need it?

For example, let's assume that you're responsible for a *Team-Building Session* for your company, but you still need a guest speaker. So, your *Unresolved Issue* might read:

"Need to identify and contract one guest speaker for the final dinner, on June 23, at our annual Team-Building Session at the Hilton Hotel no later than June 1."

Step 3. Add it to the Unresolved Issues List.

Here's a simple table for your Unresolved Issues.

Unresolved Issues List					
Date	Action Item	Who	Deadline	Status/ Date
May 4	Need to identify and contract one guest speaker for the final dinner, on June 23, at our annual Team-Building Session at the Hilton Hotel no later than June 1.	Tom	June 23	Ongoing /May 10

Notice that this table captures the date the issue was identified (May 4), the action item stated in one sentence, Tom is responsible for resolving the issue, the deadline (DL) is June 23, and the status with the date you last checked is "Ongoing/May 10." The reason for this much detail is to enable your boss and his boss to help you resolve your issues without asking you any questions.

Step 4. Provide a copy to your boss.

Always ensure your boss has a current copy of all your *Unresolved Issues*. If he doesn't have these details, he can't help you.

Step 5. Continue to eliminate each issue.

All *Unresolved Issues* should go on your list until two things happen:

- Until the answer is *known for certain*, meaning that the answer is a fact rather than an opinion or speculation.
- Until the answer is *acceptable to you*, meaning that it's no longer an issue.

Keep the issue on your list until the issue is both *"Known for Certain"* and *"Acceptable to You."*

Don't be surprised when one issue is resolved that several new issues appear. Just add them to your list and get as much help as you can to resolve each issue.

Step 6. Seek Assistance.

Also, discuss your *Unresolved Issues* during any future meetings or updates. Others at the meeting may be able to help you - but they need to know your issues.

> *Look, this technique is designed to help you get things done. No one can help you if they don't know your Unresolved Issues. So, don't let your pride or fear get in your way.*

When an issue is resolved, don't delete it from your list because you'll need it later for your *After-Action Review*. Just record it as completed. When the issue is resolved, notify your boss. The worst thing you could ever do is to conceal your Unresolved Issues from your boss.

This page is intentionally left blank.

33
BY ANTICIPATING CONSEQUENCES AND EFFECTS

"The world is moved not only by the mighty shoves of heroes, but also by the aggregate of the tiny pushes of each honest worker."
- Helen Keller

Do you know how to anticipate and mitigate anything that could produce unexpected outcomes, causing delays or stoppage to your project?

By anticipating Unintended Consequences

Unintended Consequences are outcomes that aren't the outcomes expected from your project.

Unintended Consequences fall into three categories:

- **A positive**, unexpected benefit, which is usually referred to as serendipity or a windfall.
- **A negative**, unexpected problem like irrigation providing water for agriculture could also lead to cholera.
- The consequence of **what others might say or do** is referred to as backlash, fallout, or blowback.

Here's an example of a negative Unintended Consequence.

Can you tell what's wrong with this picture? Hint: Does Starbucks really suck?

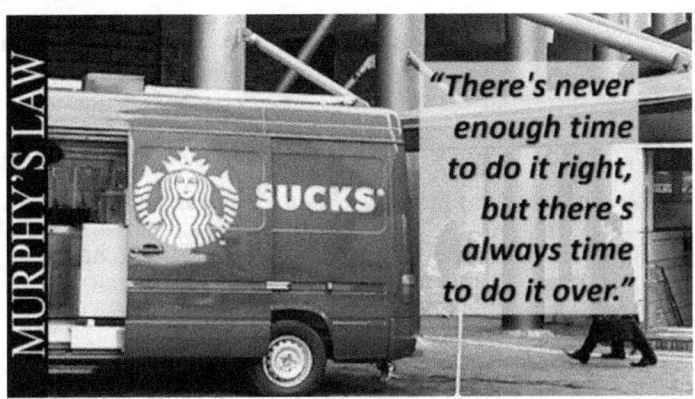

Answer: The painters applied the Starbucks advertising on a delivery van with the doors closed. Unfortunately, they failed to consider the unintended consequences of what the van would look like when the side door was open. This is *Murphy's Law* at its best!

By anticipating Second and Third-Order Effects

Be sensitive to how your work affects others.

Second and Third-Order Effects focus on how your work will affect others at different levels in your company.

Different levels mean how your work will affect others in your unit, department, company, and suppliers. *Second and Third-Order Effects* may also identify new resource requirements and cause changes to structures and procedures.

For example, if you decide to change a supplier, the effects could be extensive.

- *Second-Order Effects* could require new ordering procedures to be created, which could cause delays.
- *Third-Order Effects* could require others to be retrained on new ordering procedures and software.

To anticipate *Second and Third-Order Effects* keep asking.

Now, what? What's next? What're we forgetting? And what could happen or what might we need to do in 30, 60, or 90 days?

How can you Anticipate Anything?

You're responsible for anticipating the consequences and effects of your work before starting.

But how can you do this when your crystal ball is no less clear than mine?

Method 1: Find others who have dealt with similar problems and ask:

- What problems, consequences, or effects did you have?
- Did everything go as planned? Any do-overs or surprises?
- What outside help did you need, and where did you get it?
- Anything or anyone you didn't have before starting?

- What was the most important and the most difficult task?
- How long did each task take, and what was the cost?
- Anything you'd start, stop, or change next time?
- Was everyone satisfied with the results?

Method 2: Vendors and Suppliers.

Contact vendors and suppliers who have worked with those who have dealt with the same or similar problems and ask the questions from Method 1. Also, which city, county, or state agency must inspect the problem to see if it meets the code?

Method 3: YouTube.

Visit *YouTube* to search for related videos of others who have dealt with the same or similar problems. Then, get on social media and find people who have experienced projects or problems similar to yours. If you find someone, ask the questions from Method 1.

By making changes with CAUTION

Whenever a change is made, there are always consequences and effects. Just because everyone gets the change doesn't mean they understand it. The problem comes later when the consequences and effects start to appear, and everyone is shocked.

Here's a good example:

Bob was the Person-in-Charge of the company's Annual Team Building Session. Two days before the session, Bob's boss (the CFO) called and told him that the venue had been changed to a remote cabin where there was no electricity. Bob called John, the Key Player in-charge of food and beverages, to inform John of the change in venue and the lack of electricity.

The day before the session, Bob followed up with John and was shocked to find that John had not thought through the refrigeration requirements for the food and beverages. Since this was a three-day session, the change of venue not only required ice to be transported to the venue daily but coolers to store it.

John didn't recognize the need for ice, and Bob assumed John had it covered. As a result, the night before the session, both John and Bob spent several hours in the dark, scrambling around looking for coolers and bags of ice to fill them.

All this could have been avoided had John and Bob thought through the consequences and effects created by this last-minute change in venue by testing their assumptions and creating a Plan or Action to deal with it. Not to mention the need for a site recon and a review of the Checklist at Appendix E.

Murphy's Law on Consequences:
"There's never enough time to do it right, but there's always time to do it over."

34
BY DEMONSTRATING GOOD JUDGMENT

"Experience is simply the name we give our mistakes."
- Oscar Wilde

In your attempt to save time, do you rush and make snap decisions without considering the consequences?

Good judgment is your ability to bring together reason and wisdom to analyze a situation, explore your options, select a course of action, and take action.

Good judgment isn't about being smart or about making good decisions.

The essence of good judgment is about learning from past mistakes.

It's about using your *Assessment Systems* (Chapter 36) to ensure you don't repeat the same mistakes and increase the probability of success of your next attempt.

Judgment is less about getting it right and more about what it takes to learn what went wrong.

Some of your decisions will result in *Unintended Consequences*. To add to this uncertainty, you'll soon discover that your decisions aren't always about what's good or bad. Often, they're about choosing between good, better, and best. All decisions have consequences, which you won't see in advance. But experience teaches that they'll come due someday.

Where do good decisions come from?

Good decisions don't happen by accident.

- Good decisions come from good judgment.
- Good judgment comes from failure.
- Failure comes from mistakes.
- Mistakes come from bad decisions.

- Bad decisions come from bad judgment.
- Bad judgment comes from a lack of experience.
- Lack of experience comes from:
  - ✓ Having little time invested in the job.
  - ✓ Not learning from your mistakes.
  - ✓ Not learning from the mistakes of others.
  - ✓ Making quick decisions when you have more time.
  - ✓ A failure to venture outside your comfort zone.

Mistakes, as long as you learn from them, are the building blocks of greatness.

How can you learn from the mistakes of others?

Learning from the mistakes of others only happens if you're paying attention. There are only two ways to learn anything in life, either by trial and error or by modeling the best practices. While it's important to learn from your mistakes, it's a lot easier to learn from the mistakes of others.

How can Modeling help you?

Experience is the toughest teacher because it gives the test first and the knowledge second.

Modeling a better teacher because it gives you the knowledge, so you're better prepared for the test.

Modeling is the process of learning from those who've already achieved success.

It also means learning by copying the behavior of those who've already experienced the mistakes and failures on their journey to success (Chapter 36). You can avoid the same mistakes and failures by learning, applying, and sharing what you'll learn here. Each new skill learned builds on the previous, and the compound effect is career-changing.

35
BY KNOWING WHEN TO ACT, WAIT OR WALK AWAY

> *"You got to know when to hold 'em. Know when to fold 'em. Know when to walk away and know when to run."*
> *- Kenny Rogers, The Gambler*

When faced with a problem, how do you know what to do? For every problem you'll face, you'll normally have three choices of how to respond:

You can act, wait, or walk away.

When faced with a problem, can't you just do nothing? Sure. Think about it. You have this option every time you're faced with a problem. Do some problems sometimes correct themselves by doing nothing? Yes. Do some problems get worse by taking action rather than doing nothing? You bet!

Remember, doing nothing is deciding by default.

Are there some problems that are better left alone? Sure. Just ask any Firefighter. Most of the time, all they can do is contain the fire and just let it burn itself out; let it *burn-to-the-ground*. So if you feel this is your best choice, among all the choices you have at the time, then do nothing – let it *burn-to-the-ground*.

However, doing nothing and waiting are two different options.

When faced with any problem, use these steps to guide your response.

Step 1: Should I Act NOW?

Before deciding, answer these questions?

- Can this problem be resolved by calling 911? If Yes, call!
- Will acting now save lives or avoid further damage?
  - ✓ If Yes, take *Immediate Action* (Appendix F).
  - ✓ If No to both questions, continue to Step 2.

Step 2: Is this my problem?

Is this my problem or someone else's?

- Who has the most to gain or lose from its resolution?
- Who's affected by this problem?

If this problem isn't your problem, why are you trying to solve it? Just report it to your boss and walk away. If this is your problem, continue to the next step.

Step 3: Should I act now or wait?

How urgent is this problem?

- How important or urgent is this problem and why?
- What must happen before I'm forced to act?
- What are the consequences if this problem remains unresolved?
- What's the downside of waiting?

How much time do I have?

- How long do I have before this problem becomes a crisis?
- How long do I have before I'm forced to act?
- When's it too late to act?

Based on your answers to the above questions, use the *Decision Support Template* below to guide your decision.

Here's an example of a *Decision Support Template*: Time vs. Urgency.

Decision Support Matrix		Time to Decide?	
		Little Time	Enough Time
Urgency?	Urgent	1	2
	Not Urgent	3	4

Here's what the numbers mean:
1. If this problem is urgent and you have little time to decide, take *Immediate Action* (Appendix F) and develop a mental *Plan of Action* before acting (Appendix B). See CONPLAN 1.
2. If this problem is urgent and you have enough time, take Step 4. Prepare to act after completing your *Plan of Action*. Keep your boss informed. See CONPLAN 2.
3. If this problem isn't urgent and you have little time to decide, wait, continue to monitor the situation, create your *Plan of Action*, and keep your boss informed. See CONPLAN 3.
4. If this problem isn't urgent and you have enough time to act, continue to monitor the situation, create your *Plan of Action*, and update your boss. See CONPLAN 4.

Also, document what happened, when, and who took action to resolve the problem for investigative or legal purposes later.

Step 4: Create your Plan of Action.

See Appendix B.

Note: You're responsible for anticipating the consequences and effects (Chapter 33) of your work BEFORE deciding.

Other Things to Consider

When's the best time to decide?

> *"The key is not to make quick decisions,*
> *but to make timely decisions."*
> *- Colin Powell*

Do you have to make the decision right now? This classic answer is usually, No! This is rarely necessary. Resist the impulse of making a snap decision when there's no need to do so. Normally, you'll have sufficient time to decide.

A good rule of thumb is to decide after acquiring **40-70%** of the information you need. Mistakes, as long as you learn from them, are the building blocks of greatness. If it turns out bad, adjust, and remember what you've learned for next time.

Who's the Best Person to decide?

First, the boss decides! Or, at least, the boss should take responsibility and ownership of his team's decisions, especially if it turns out bad. Ask members for their input before you decide. Also, if the decision affects everyone in your team, why can't all members be given a chance to concur or non-concur with reasons (Chapter 24)?

Does the Best Decision always produce the Best Outcome?

There's a big difference between your decision and the result or outcome of your decision. You could be the most experienced decision-maker on the planet, and you could make the best decision, but there's no guarantee that your problem will be resolved or the best outcome will be achieved. You can make a good decision, and the results could still be bad. The situation and facts available when you first decided could (and probably will) change over time. What was good today could turn out to be bad tomorrow.

Do you need your Boss's Approval?

Have you ever been in a situation where you were waiting for your boss's approval? Why are you asking for approval if the problem is internal, doesn't require additional resources you don't have, and isn't in conflict with any internal standards? That's what your boss is paying you to do. But do let him know.

Sometimes it's easier to ask forgiveness than permission.

Or, if you're in doubt, tell your boss when you'll be making your decision (like the end of the week), and if you don't hear from him before that time, you'll be moving forward. Don't forget to assess the consequences and effects of your actions.

What if a Direct Reports recommends a change?

One of the best bosses I ever worked with once said,

> **"If I can't give you a good reason not to make the change; I'll approve it."**

Yes, they still had to create a *Decision Paper* (Appendix C), build consensus with the team (Chapter 24), and present it to the team for a final discussion before approval. However, this gave the team the freedom they needed to make things better.

36
BY LEARNING FROM MISTAKES AND FAILURE

"If you're not making mistakes, then you're not doing anything. I'm positive that a doer makes mistakes."
- John Wooden

Will you make mistakes and have failures in your lifetime? You bet lots of them. But that's how we all learn. So, how can you learn from mistakes and failure? Effective people know that the only thing that matters is what you learn for the next time regarding mistakes and failure.

What's Failure?

The dictionary defines failure as:

"The state or condition of not meeting a desirable or intended goal and may be viewed as the opposite of success."

Failure is a relative term. It's viewed differently depending on your situation and who's doing the viewing. For example, failure to a baseball player may be striking out, but failure to his coach might be losing the game.

In the Business World, your goals will come from your boss. Did you accomplish the goals (Chapter 16) you were assigned? Did you achieve the result you wanted? If not, why?

The only important question is, what did you learn that can make you better next time? I used to think that there was no such thing as failure (it didn't exist) if you never gave up. But this is only partially true and sends the wrong message.

You'll experience mistakes and failures in your life. The trick is not to let them define you.

Instead, let them Refine you and make you stronger!

The past doesn't equal the future. So, learn what you need to learn and move on!

What's the difference between a failure and an unsuccessful attempt?

- **Failure** needs a substantial loss (like money, time, or reputation).
- An **Unsuccessful Attempt** means that your last attempt did not achieve the desired result.

However, if you can make another attempt, did you learn why the last attempt was unsuccessful? Do you know what changes need to be made for your next attempt to be successful?

Failure only exists if there's a loss.
The bigger the loss, the bigger the failure.

The example most often used comes from the story of ***Thomas Edison*** and his 10,000 attempts to create the incandescent light bulb. Just remember, *Edison* could make as many attempts as he needed until he was successful because he wasn't paying for each attempt. His investors were paying the bills. Most people don't have that luxury.

What's Failure in the Real World?

There are two types of failure which are commonly misunderstood:

- **Personal failure:** This is an unsuccessful attempt at accomplishing your personal goal (Chapter 36) and includes a:
  - ✓ **Failure to try.** This means never setting goals or never attempting to accomplish anything.
  - ✓ **Failure to keep trying.** This means that after an unsuccessful initial attempt, you failed to learn from your mistakes, make the changes needed, find a different way to get there, or make another attempt.
  - ✓ **Substantial Loss.** This is a loss of your wealth, relationships, health, *character, or reputation.
- **Company failure:** This is a failure to accomplish an assigned goal, resulting in losing anything your boss couldn't afford to lose.

*To learn more about ***Character***, available at **Amazon.com**, see page 5.

Let's examine what should happen BEFORE you attempt to accomplish any goal.

Before the Attempt

Step 1. What's the Risk?

Conduct a *Risk Assessment* to look for all the things that could reasonably go wrong during your attempt. Then, collaborate to assess all your safety, security, financial, and operational risk and how they can be mitigated.

Step 2. How many attempts?

If you know you'll only get one attempt, make it count! But, on the other hand, if you know you'll get as many attempts as you need, then the only risk is the cost of each additional attempt. Remember ***Edison***?

Step 3. What's the cost?

- **Cost:** What will it cost to make this attempt (how much time, money, or effort will it take)?
- **Opportunity Costs:** What are you losing by not using other alternatives?

Step 4. What if you're wrong?

Can everyone live with an unsuccessful attempt?

Step 5. What are the benefits?

What benefits will you receive if your attempt is successful?

Step 6. Is the benefit worth the cost?

- **If Yes:** Continue to create your *Plan of Action*.
- **If No or Unsure:** Work hard to mitigate your Risk. Then, conduct another Cost/Benefit Analysis.

Step 7. What's your Assessment System?

An *Assessment System* is a series of procedures designed to measure the most critical parameters of your attempt to determine what went wrong, right, and why? How will the attempt be measured? How do you know when it's time to *pull-the-plug?*

An Assessment System is a combination of targeted, proactive procedures designed to identify problems before they occur and resolve problems once identified.

This system is called CAPA (Corrective Actions, Preventive Actions) and should be part of your overall Quality Management System (QMS) and includes procedures to prevent problems (PA) and procedures to correct problems (CA) once identified.

Mistakes or defects are not a problem if they're identified and resolved before your boss or customer discovers them.

After the Attempt

Let's examine what should happen AFTER your attempt.

Step 8. Was the attempt a complete success?

- **If Yes:** Congrats! What's next?
- **If No:** If your attempt was unsuccessful, was there a loss?
    - ✓ If there was NO loss, what did you learn, and what changes need to be made? Never give up! Just find another way to get there.
    - ✓ If there was a loss, now you have a real failure. The greater the loss, the greater the failure.

Step 9. What did you learn from your Assessment System?

- What went wrong, right, and why?
- What needs to change to make your next attempt a success?
- How will you know when it's time to *pull-the-plug?*

The lesson may have been painful, but don't throw the learning away. istakes and failures can be your best teacher, but only if you remember the lesson. Now what? Well, that depends on you!

Is Failure Fatal?

"Failure is not fatal, but failure to change might be."
- John Wooden

Assuming your attempt resulted in a loss, it's not the end of your life or your career. And, sometimes, getting close is good enough. So assess what happened, what you learned, and get *back-in-the-game!*

Never give up! Just find another way to get there.

Never Stop Learning!

Can you achieve Success without Failure?

"If things are not failing, you are not innovating enough."
- Elon Musk

For all of **Elon Musk's** success, he has experienced an equal amount of failure. Whatever future success he achieves will most likely be accompanied by more failure.

Here are three times **Elon Musk** failed:

1. Once, he couldn't get a CEO job to save his life.

When **Zip2** began attracting investors, they stripped him of his role as Chairman. Musk's idea of leadership in the 1990s was to stay late and rewrite code, believing his employees were incompetent. He failed to see how publicly berating his employees might make them less productive.

2. He has crashed more than his share of rockets.

SpaceX, 2002, his career serves as ample proof that the first step to success is a whole bunch of failures. It wasn't until April 8, 2016, that the company managed the first of three consecutive successful landings. Unfortunately, the results in June resulted in four rocket launches in a row ending in flames.

3. He has never delivered a car on time.

Tesla revealed that it built only 260 Model 3 vehicles, instead of the promised 1,500, with no chance of making the originally claimed 5,000 by the end of the year. Shipments were initially expected to begin in 2013, yet the first cars didn't ship until late 2015.

By comparison, it took *Amazon* more than 14 years to make as much profit as it produced the previous quarter. *Amazon* consistently lost money for its first several years as a public company.

Lessons Learned: Constantly seek criticism and feedback; it's as good as gold! Never give up. Just find another way to get there.

> *"Being an entrepreneur starting up is like eating glass and staring into the abyss of death."*
> *- Unknown*

37
BY ASSESSING PERFORMANCE

"Followership, like leadership, is a role and not a destination."
- Michael McKinney

Do you know how to measure the performance of members, teams, and systems to enhance their ability to consistently produce excellent results?

Are they getting better or worse? How do you know for sure? Your performance includes your results, behavior, and potential.

Effective people don't just set the bar; they are the bar.

Are they getting better or worse? How do you know for sure?

What's the best way to measure performance?

The best way to measure performance is by using solid, objective measurements. Actual performance measurement is a more effective way to evaluate results because the measurement is relevant to the situation or process. Some of the best ways to assess performance are by using *Metrics, Objectives and Key Results (OKRs)*, *Key Performance Indicators (KPIs), and Bands of Excellence (BOEs)*.

By using Metrics

Metrics are quantifiable and allow you to set the <u>desired</u> result compared to the <u>actual</u> result, but there's a downside.

A metric is something used to measure and track the results of members, teams, or systems to assess its performance.

Here's a good story:

Bob was assigned to improve the number of "problem fixes per day" called into the Helpdesk in his company. He spent a few hours in the Helpdesk Call Center to observe. To his amazement, he found that each Helpdesk Operator was assessed daily using 17 different metrics. For example, one metric was how much "time the operator spent on the phone."

The operators were told to keep each call to less than two minutes, which was counterproductive in solving the caller's problems. After a few hours, Bob determined that working under these conditions (metrics) was not where he wanted to work. His intuition told him that the metrics were too restrictive. So, he directed that all metrics be stopped except for one; the number of "problems fixed per day."

Result? The number of *"problems fixed per day"* shot up off the charts. Problem solved! So, be careful with all your metrics. Sometimes less is more. Focus on the most important metrics – the ones that make sense.

Here are some typical metrics.

- **Cash Flow:** Cash flow is the money coming in and out of your business on any given day, which is what you use to cover your business expenses, such as payroll, rent, and inventory.
- **Customer: Customer Acquisition Cost (CAC).** Divide your total acquisition costs by the number of new customers over the same time frame you're examining.
- **Employee: Employee Turnover Rate (ETR).** To determine your ETR, take the number of employees who have departed the company and divide it by the average number of employees. If you have a high ETR, spend some time examining your workplace culture, employment packages, and work environment.

By using Objectives and Key Results (OKRs)

An OKR (or Objectives and Key Results) is a framework for defining and tracking objectives and their outcomes.

OKR is generally attributed to **Andy Grove**, CEO of Intel, who introduced the approach to Intel during his tenure there and documented this in his 1983 book *High Output Management*. OKRs comprise an **O**bjective, a clearly defined goal, and one or more **K**ey **R**esults (specific measures used to track the achievement of that objective).

OKRs:

- May be shared across the company to provide teams with visibility of goals to align and focus effort.

- Are typically set at the company, team, and personal levels, although there is criticism on this causing too much of a waterfall approach, which OKRs try to be the opposite in many ways.
- Overlap with other performance management frameworks - complexity sitting somewhere between KPI and the balanced scorecard.

The idea took hold, and OKRs quickly became central to Google's culture as a "management methodology" that helps ensure that the company focuses effort on the same important issues.

Since becoming popular at Google, OKR has favored several similar tech start-ups, including LinkedIn, Twitter, and Uber. For more on OKRs, review the book or audiobook, *Measure What Matters* by **John Doerr**.

By using Key Performance Indicators (KPI)

KPIs provide a company with a focus for strategic and operational improvement and compare achievements to similar companies.

A Key Performance Indicator (KPI) is a performance measure that demonstrates how effectively a company is at achieving its key objectives.

To be effective, a *KPI* must be well-defined and quantifiable, communicated throughout your company, crucial to achieving the goal, and applicable to the business.

Here's the difference between a *Metric* and a *KPI*?

- *KPIs* support business goals and objectives.
- *Metrics* support *KPIs* and focus on the overall tactical business goals and objectives.

Meaningful performance measures start with measurable goals. This means that your goal needs to be clear enough that you can imagine how you'll recognize it when it becomes real. So, you might first want to check if your current goals are measurable. Members won't *buy-in* to something they don't understand, weren't involved with, and see no relevance.

The key to deriving *KPIs* from objectives is to work backward and reverse engineer the *metrics* you want to create. This process is called goal, question, metric. Your objectives are your goals for your business or project (Chapter 37).

By using Bands of Excellence (BOE)

Since *Public-Sector Organizations,* like teachers or government workers, don't focus on profit generation, what matters most to their survival is providing a service that serves the greater good (like schools and government agencies). But how do they do that? They use a metric called a *Band of Excellence (or BOE)* to measure and assess their level of services. Those who work in the Public-Sector must maintain their *Band of Excellence (BOE)* set by their organization. Think of *BOEs* as the desired Standard of Performance for members, units, and systems.

A Band of Excellence is a set of performance limits ranging from the Minimum (or Standard) performance limit to the Maximum performance limit.

The difference between the minimum and the maximum is called the *Band of Excellence*. If your performance stays within the *Band of Excellence*, you remain employable.

Here's a simple example.

The biggest government agency on the planet is the US Department of Defense. In 1992, as a former US Army Officer, here's the BOE used to measure physical fitness by taking the Annual Physical Fitness Test.

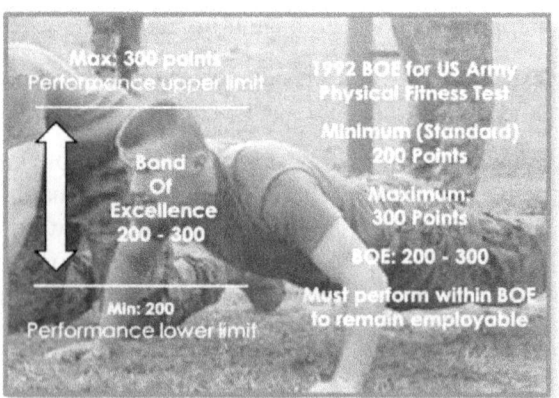

The BOE Minimum (or Standard) was 200 points overall. The BOE Maximum was 300 points overall. Therefore, the BOE was 200 - 300 for the test overall to remain promotable. If a Soldier failed to achieve 200 points overall, he was retrained and retested. If he failed a second time, he was considered un-promotable and administratively processed for release from the military.

By Tracking Trends

Have you ever tried to measure how you and your unit were doing? If not, you will. In every viable business, key metrics help determine the answer to one simple question: Are we getting better *Over-Time*?

Over-time means as compared to a past time (last month or year).

And ask the same question about yourself, *are you getting better over-time?* And your business unit, *is my business unit getting better over-time?* But how can you tell?

Here's a good example:

Think of *KPIs* as your Doctor does when you go for a physical.

- **Step 1:** What gets measured? They measure the most important aspects of optimum health, like weight, height, blood pressure, pulse, temperature, and cholesterol.

- **Step 2:** If this is your first physical, how do your numbers compare to a healthy person your age (what's the norm, standard, or benchmark)? Any corrective action needed?

- **Step 3:** If this is not your first physical, how do your numbers compare to your last physical? Are you (your physical system) getting better *over-time*? Any corrective action needed?

Use this same process with all your *Key Performance Indicators*. What are the things you can measure that tell you about the health of your unit?

Are you getting better over-time?

If not, why? What can be done (corrective action) to reverse the numbers? What number is acceptable to you? What are your standards? If this number rises above or falls below a certain level, what corrective action must be taken? Trends.

One way to visually track your *KPIs* is to measure and compare your numbers *over-time*, the trend. What does the trend look like? Is it trending in the right direction? By doing so, you'll be able to see if the trend is getting better or worse.

Here's an example of Tracking Trends.

Accounts Receivable, 90-Days Past Due (As of June 21, 20XX)			
This month	Last month	2-Months ago	1-Year Ago
$15,335	$12,457	$10,237	$25,936

Notice that this table is tracking a *Key Performance Indicator* that measures *Accounts Receivable over 90 days*. Therefore, the status ("This Month") is greater than last month and the month before. In other words, your *90-Day Past Due* numbers are increasing or getting worse.

Tip: Check your unit's usage rate or consumption rate metrics *over-time* and see what you learn.

38
BY CREATING MORE EFFECTIVE TEAM MEMBERS

"The final test of a leader is that he leaves behind him in other men, the conviction and the will to carry on."
- Walter Lippmann

Effective people set high expectations, training goals that stretch their members, and train each member at least weekly to achieve their true potential. What follows is a suggested process. Make changes as you see fit based on your specific situation.

Based on your assessment of your team's training needs, you determine that one of your most critical training tasks is to enhance your team's ability to resolve problems without your help. For this training to be effective, it should be conducted at least twice a year, until everyone can demonstrate the task to standard. Training should be mandatory and conducted at the same time every week, 1 PM Wednesday's.

This training, if conducted every week, will strengthen both the member and the team. You decide to prepare a Decision Paper (Appendix C) because it combines Critical Reasoning and Creative Thinking (Appendix G). You intend to use the *Adult Learning Model* (Chapter 8) as your method of training.

By Setting your Goals

They prepare their members by setting these goals:

- Meet or exceed their goals and demonstrate a Commitment to Purpose (Chapter 17).
- Learn, apply, and train others on the eleven *Core Competencies of Effectiveness*.
- Treat everyone with respect and kindness.
- Demonstrate a constant and never-ending sense of improvement.
- Demonstrate competence, confidence, and teamwork.
- Demonstrate a strong sense of Responsibility and Accountability (Appendix H).

- Think, write, and speak using Creative Thinking and Critical Reasoning (Appendix G).

By Training your Members

Training your members to become more effective isn't as daunting as it might seem. It begins with tasks that are critical to the success of your unit. For example, teaching your members how to write, speak, and think better can only be achieved by assigning them to write, speak, and think by assignment. This should be done at least weekly.

The First Week, Phase 1: Explain

Provide each team member with a sample format for a Decision Paper (Appendix C), a handout on Critical Reasoning and Creative Thinking (Appendix G), a copy of the Problem-Solving Process (Appendix D), and a copy of this Enabling Learning Objective:

ELO 1: Prepare a Decision Paper

Action: Prepare a Decision Paper

Condition: Given a copy of this ELO 1, a format for a Decision Paper (Appendix C), a simulated problem situation to resolve (from you), and handouts on the *Problem-Solving Process, and Critical Reasoning and Creative Thinking.

Standard: Provide a written Decision Paper, answering all applicable questions, in no more than two type-written pages, with any necessary material as enclosures, within 24 hours.

Explain and discuss each handout and how it should be used. Ensure everyone understands the Enabling Learning Objective and why you selected it. Finally, discuss what will happen over the next few weeks.

Also, explain that the Standard is GO vs. NO-GO, which means that those members who fail to meet the standard will be retested every week until they receive a GO.

*To learn more about *Problem-Solving*, available at **Amazon.com,** see page 5.

The Second Week, Phase 2: Demonstrate.

Present a simulated problem situation to the team. Lead your team through a problem-solving session using the eight steps of the Problem-Solving Process (PSP) to resolve this simulated situation. Next, verbally present your Decision Paper to the team. Provide a sample Decision Paper that you prepared for each team member. After presenting your paper, ask them to assess the Decision Paper. Ensure everyone makes an assessment.

Now, tell them what's wrong with your Decision Paper (you intentionally left out - to see who would catch it). Give them the assignment to prepare a Decision Paper based on a new simulated situation (that you provide as a handout) for next week's training. Tell them that you will select one member to present their Decision Paper next week, and another member will be selected to assess the Decision Paper.

The Third Week, Phase 3: Practice.

Ask them each at random to present their Decision Paper. Then, ask a second member to assess the presentation. Now, provide your assessment. Continue until everyone has presented and assessed. In the end, give them the assignment to prepare a Decision Paper based on a new simulated situation (that you provide as a handout) for the testing next week. Tell them that you will select one member at random to present their Decision Paper next week, and another member will be selected to assess the Decision Paper.

The Fourth Week, Phase 4: Testing and Phase 5: Assessing.

- **Testing:** Select one team member at random to present their Decision Paper to the team.

- **Assessing:** At the end of this presentation, select a different team member to assess the Decision Paper. Provide feedback to both the presenter and the assessor as to how well they used the process. Finally, collect and grade each Decision Paper and return them to each member.

At the end of the training, provide the team with another simulated problem situation to resolve. Continue this process until you are satisfied that all members can demonstrate the ELO task to standard. Repeat Quarterly, Semi-annually, or Annually, as needed.

Every Week after that, Phase 6: Training

When trained, assign each team member the additional duty of training the team on a specific ELO task according to the team's Proficiency Cycle (Quarterly, Semi-annual, or Annual). Every critical ELO should have its own designated trainer (team member) ready to present the training as scheduled. Repeat this process for every critical ELO task and document who met which ELO task and the date they were last tested.

Each team member is expected to be able to respond to a simulated (or actual) problem situation using common sense, their training, and the tools you've provided.

In the end, this entire experience is designed for the member (not for you), so they can have the confidence they need to function on their own. Your job is to guide and encourage them to improve with every lesson, without getting in their way! You are preparing them to WIN!

Caution: Be careful with your internal competition (Appendix A).

APPENDIX A: USE INTERNAL COMPETITION

Have you ever played a game and observed the teamwork brought about by friendly competition? First, it's hard to find any athletic competition that's truly friendly. Second, in most cases, this competition was focused more on member performance than on team performance. This is why some professional athletes get multi-million-dollar contracts, and others don't.

Here are three approaches to <u>Team Member Competition</u>:

- **Approach 1:** Compete by pitting one member against another. Here you'll have one *loser* and one *winner*. Unfortunately, this form of competition can destroy team cohesion and cooperation.

- **Approach 2:** Compete by pitting one member's results (monthly sales $$) against every other member on the team and publishing the results at the end of the month (rank-ordered from "most sales" at the top and "least sales" at the bottom). While this can be motivating for some, it could erode teamwork.

- **Approach 3:** Compete by pitting one member against a goal that he set for himself. Here the competition is against the standard, trying to beat their *last-personal-best*.

Here are two approaches to <u>Team Competition</u>:

- **Approach 1:** Compete by pitting one team against another. Here you still have one *winner* and one *loser*. However, playing against the best is the only way to elevate your game and improve. This may work great on the athletic field but probably won't work well in business.

- **Approach 2:** Compete by pitting the entire team against goals they've set for themselves. This is the kind of competition you're looking for in a real team. But, again, this breeds cooperation and teamwork.

Which approach is Best?

It depends on your situation. Who produces the results: the team or member? Are you more concerned with teamwork or member contributions?

- **Teamwork:** Since cooperation is what holds great teams together, have your team compete against a goal that they've set for themselves (collectively) and not against each other (so you don't have one *winner* and one *loser*).

- **Member:** Have the member compete against a goal that he has set for himself (his *last-personal-best*) and not against another member.

Note: To be effective, these goals, created by the member or team, must be measurable and contribute to the boss's goals. Also, if the team or member consistently exceeds their goals, they should be recognized.

B
CREATE A PLAN OF ACTION

Here's a real-world example of a *Plan of Action*.

Situation: Using *Role-Playing*, let's assume your name is Bob, and it's May 1, 20XX. You've just been told by your boss (the Director of IT) that you're the Project Manager for the Company Picnic on June 21st.

This means that you're *in-charge*, so *Take-Charge* by completing your draft POA. You visited the picnic site, and you've spoken to last year's Project Manager and learned that it rained last year, and everyone was soaked. Also, from last year's survey results, you learned that the only condiment was ketchup.

You're the Manager of IT within your company. You have five Direct Reports. Each Direct Report has five entry-level team members that report to them. You decide that there are five main tasks to be performed to make the picnic a success:

- Prepare and serve picnic food and drink.
- Provide entertainment.
- Present awards.
- Conduct youth activities.
- Conduct picnic clean-up.

But who should be assigned to perform these tasks?

During your *Backbriefing,* you present these options to your boss:

Option 1: You could contract out some of the work. However, your boss has already told you that this will be done internally.

Option 2: You could perform all major tasks yourself. You quickly realize that the sheer scope of the assignment would cause you to be overwhelmed.

Option 3: You could share the load by assigning one major task to each of the other major units within the company. Your boss disagrees and reminds you that you don't have assignment authority outside your IT Unit. But nice try!

Option 4: You could assign these five tasks to your five Direct Reports. You decide to take this option because you and your boss agree that this is the best of the four options available.

DRAFT *PLAN OF ACTION* (POA) FOR A COMPANY PICNIC

Subject: Draft *Plan of Action* for Company Picnic, June 21, 20XX

Objective: ABC Company (Who) conducts their annual picnic (What) on June 21, 20XX, from 12:00 to 4:30 PM (When), at Mason Park, Lot 14, (Where) to improve morale, have fun, get to know each other, and celebrate our accomplishments (Why - Purpose). If it rains, the picnic will move to the Jefferson High School Gymnasium.

Methods: (How)

Concept: ABC Picnic will be conducted in three phases:

Phase 1: Set-up of food, entertainment, and activities begin at 10 AM at Mason Park.

Phase 2: The picnic will begin at noon and end at 4:30 PM.

Phase 3: Clean-up will begin at 4:30 PM until finished.

Specific Instructions:

Key Players	Major Tasks	Jun 21 @	Notes
Bill	Set up and run youth activities	NLT 12:00	See Youth Activities enclosure
John	Clean-up picnic site	4:30 PM	Bring trash bags
Lisa	Provide musical entertainment	12:00 to 4:30 PM	See Entertainment enclosure
Joe	Prepare and serve picnic meal.	Serve NLT 12:00	See Picnic Menu enclosure. Ensure plenty of condiments!
Mary Anne	Prepare/present awards	Present at 1 PM	See Awards enclosure. Rehearsal on June 20, 1 PM in our conference room

General Instructions: Dress is casual. Bring plenty of sunscreen and either blanket or folding chairs to sit on.

Risk:

Safety: Bring plenty of Sunscreen.

Security: Lock your car and do not leave valuables in your car.

Financial: N/A

Assumptions: Headcount will be the same as last year (150 people).

Timetable: See enclosure 2 (Timetable)

Resources Needed:

Who (Unit)	What	Where	Jun 21 @
Joe	4-Folding tables for food, 3-Grills	Lot 14, Mason Park	NLT 11:30
Mary Anne	Public Address system	Lot 14, Mason Park	NLT 11:30
Bill	Youth Game Equipment	Lot 14, Mason Park	NLT 11:30

Unresolved Issues: See enclosure 1 (*Unresolved Issues List*)

FOR THE DIRECTOR:

Your Signature:

Project Manager: Bob Murray, email, and phone number.

Distribution: 1-Each Key Player, 1-Your Boss, 1-File

Enclosures:

1: *Unresolved Issues List (Enclosure 1)*

2: *Timetable (Enclosure 2)*

3: Program Schedule (To Be Published)

4: Changes (TBP)

5: Youth Activities (TBP)

6: Picnic Menu (TBP)

7: Awards (TBP)

Enclosure 1: *Unresolved Issues List*

Unresolved Issue List					
Date	Unresolved Issue	Assigned	Deadline	Checked	Status
~~May 4~~	~~Which youth games?~~	~~Bill~~	~~May 6~~		~~Answered~~
May 5	No money is available	Joe	May 7		On-going
Don't delete anything from this list. You'll need them later. Just ~~Strike Through~~ them when they are both <u>known</u> and <u>acceptable to you</u>.					

Enclosure 2: *Timetable*:

Partial Timetable for Company Picnic (June 21)							
Yr	M	D	Time	Preventive Actions	Responsible	Where	Who
14	5	2	1 PM	Site visit conducted	Bob	B	
14	5	4	2 PM	Backbriefing	Bob	A	
14	5	4		Advanced Warning	Bob		
14	5	6		Draft POA Staffed	Bob		
14	5	10		Final Decision Briefing	Bob	A	2
14	5	12		Final POA distributed	Bob		
14	5	25	2 PM	IPR #1: Milestone 1	All	A	2
14	6	1		Promotion begins	Bob		
14	6	1		Request resources	Joe		
14	6	14	2 PM	IPR #2: Milestone 2	All	A	2
14	6	19	1 PM	Final site visit	Bob	B	2
14	6	20		Buy Food & Drinks	Joe		
14	6	20	1 PM	Rehearsals	Bob	A	2
14	6	21	10 AM	Equipment set-up	Joe	B	2
14	6	21	12:00	Company Picnic	All	B	1
14	6	22	12:0	After-Action Review	All	B	1

Understanding how to create a *Plan of Action* will help you move your work forward and enhance your credibility with your boss.

C
CREATE A DECISION PAPER

Have you ever been asked to write a *Decision Paper or a Business Case*? If not, you will. This is one way your boss is preparing you for the next level.

The purpose of a *Decision Paper* or a *Business Case* is to persuade a Decision-Maker to spend the money needed to move your work forward. A Decision-Maker is the person who controls the money and may be several levels above you.

Sometimes you'll need resources that you don't have, like people, equipment, or facilities, to solve a problem – which means spending money. When this happens, you'll need the DM's approval before moving forward. To persuade anyone to accept your recommendation, you'll need a well-written *Decision Paper,* and here's a great format.

What's the best format to use to create a Decision Paper?

    1. Subject. Briefly state the subject.

    2. Problem. State the problem in one sentence.

    3. Recommendation. State the recommended solution in one sentence.

    4. Benefits: State the expected benefits of this recommendation.

    5. Key Player Comments.

    A Key Player is anyone whose opinion would matter to the Decision-Maker or anyone who'll be required to support the recommendation if approved. You'll need to *Staff* your paper through all Key Players for their concurrence or non-concurrence with comments (Chapter 24). Once comments are returned, create a table showing which Key Players concurred or non-concurred with their reasons.

    6. Discussion. Explain why you're recommending this solution by answering these questions.

- **What were all the solutions you considered?** Then, attach all the solutions you considered with all the Advantages and Disadvantages.
- **Why did you select this solution?**

- **What's the cost and who should pay?**

- **What's the Risk?** How probable is this risk, how severe will it be, and how can it be mitigated (Chapters 26-28). If a *Contingency Plan* is needed, add it as an enclosure (Chapter 29).

- **How long will it take, and when should it be started?**

- **How long do we have before this problem becomes a crisis?**

- **What are the consequences and effects of this recommendation?** *Unintended Consequences* are outcomes that are not expected from your project. *2nd and 3rd Order Effects* deal with how your project affects others, like those in your company or your suppliers (Chapter 33).

- **What are the *Unresolved Issues*?** Attach a list of all the questions, unknowns, concerns, shortfalls, obstacles, and problems that could slow or stop your progress (Chapter 32).

- **What are all the Facts and Assumptions?** Attach a list of all the facts and assumptions you used.

When your paper is finished, give a Decision Briefing or provide a hard copy to the DM to gain approval. If you choose this option, ensure your paper is no more than two pages in length, with all the supporting documents attached as enclosures.

What's a Business Case?

A *Decision Paper* is also known as a *Business Case*, which is the justification to convince a Decision-Maker to accept a proposal.

A Business Case is a document that captures the reasons for initiating an action.

The logic is that whenever resources are consumed, they should support a specific business need. For example, it could be a software upgrade needed to improve system performance. The "business case" is that a software upgrade would improve customer satisfaction, require less task processing time, or reduce system maintenance costs. A compelling business case should capture both the quantifiable and non-quantifiable characteristics of the proposed action.

Creating a *Decision Paper* or a *Business Case* is a great way to convince your boss to accept your recommendation and enhance your credibility.

D
REAL WORLD PROBLEM-SOLVING EXAMPLE

For all those who appreciate the ability to decide with confidence, this is for you.

Here's a real-world example of the *Problem-Solving Process* in Action.

Situation: Using *Role-Playing*, let's assume you are the IT Director for a $3 Billion Telecom Supplier. You and your team have decided to update your IT infrastructure because you've outgrown your current system. You provided a Decision Briefing to your boss, and he agreed to the upgrade. But he stated that no more than $150,000 would be available for the upgrade. Your team has already completed the requirements document, you approved it, and your boss has agreed to fund the work.

You intend to use the *Problem-Solving Process* to select the BEST Vendor.

Step 1:
Define the Problem

In your search for the Best Vendor, you continued to capture and eliminate all *Unresolved Issues* (Chapter 32).

Being more of a *Supportive - Delegating Style* Project Manager, you're comfortable asking your team to concur or non-concur with reasons after each step of the process to confirm whether they can support the work thus far. Any non-concurring reasons are presented to the group for resolution.

Assignment: Select the BEST Vendor.

In this situation, your problem statement is:

Which is the best vendor to update our IT infrastructure?

Step 2:
Gather Information

Facts: The requirements document is completed (stating the capabilities needed) and approved by your boss. Your boss has agreed to fund the upgrade to a limit of $150,000.

Assumptions: That the Vendors considered are the only Vendors capable of performing the work.

At the end of Day 1, you assembled your team and asked them to either concur or non-concur (with reasons) on the results of Steps 1 and 2. Non-concurring reasons were resolved within the team. After some open and candid discussion, all 5-team members (your team members) concurred that they could follow, support, and execute the work thus far, so the process could move forward. In your pursuit of the BEST Vendor, you continued to focus on your *Unresolved Issues List*.

Step 3:
List Possible Solutions

Since you decided to conduct a *Brainstorming* session to determine the BEST Vendor to do the work, you gave your team the following instructions before they all left for the day.

> *"Tomorrow morning, we'll be conducting a Brainstorming session to determine the BEST vendor to update our IT infrastructure. When you get home tonight, I need each of you to come up with as many vendors as you can that could potentially make this happen. Tomorrow, when we meet, I will ask each of you to tell me which vendors you've selected and why. Please don't share your selections with other team members before the Brainstorming session. See you tomorrow back here at 8 AM, ready to go."*

You've already collected some large sheets on a vertical easel to write on during the session (so everyone can see their suggestions up on the walls), masking tape, and wide-tipped, black markers to record their input.

You decided to facilitate the *Brainstorming* session. You also assigned one of your team members as the scribe to record each recommendation.

After 20-minutes, 11-Vendors were identified, and an open discussion began.

You and your team, using the *Common-Sense Test*, eliminated any Vendor that wasn't:

- Suitable (does it solve the problem, and is it legal and ethical)?
- Feasible (fits within available or reasonably acquirable resources)?
- Acceptable (worth the cost or risk)?
- Distinguishable (differs significantly from other solutions)?
- Complete (can solve the problem from start to finish)?

As a result, the original group of 11-Vendors was reduced to 10 because one Vendor couldn't COMPLETE the installation from start to finish. So now, only 10-Vendors remain. But which vendor is BEST? This could only be answered by rank ordering all possible solutions, from BEST to Worst, and testing each solution.

At this point, you asked your team to either concur or non-concur with the work completed thus far. Non-concurring reasons were resolved within the team. After some open and candid discussion, all members concurred that they could follow, execute, and support the results thus far, so the process could move forward. In your pursuit of the BEST Vendor, you continued to focus on your *Unresolved Issues List*.

The next day, you assembled your team again to determine your *Screening and Evaluative Criteria*.

Step 4:
Test Possible Solutions

Step 4.1: Determine Screening and Evaluative Criteria:

Screening Criteria: Since your boss capped his funding at $150,000 for the update, and you had $50,000 from your budget dedicated to IT Infrastructure, you and your team decided to eliminate any Vendor with a total cost greater than $200,000. Also, any Vendor that could not meet all requirements from the requirements document was screened out (eliminated).

Formula: You and your team decided that the lowest score would win (like a game of Golf).

Evaluative Criteria: You and your team struggled to define what "BEST Vendor" meant. After much discussion, you and your team were comfortable with 3-Criterion; Total cost, Time to install, and Number of positive referrals. In your pursuit of the BEST Vendor, you continued to focus on your *Unresolved Issues List*.

Note: Here, you'll notice that COST was used as both a *screening and evaluative criterion*.

Weighting: You and your team had 3-Evaluative Criteria that made sense and discussed the weighting of the Evaluative Criterion from Most Important or Least Important and agreed to this weighting:

- **Most Important:** Total Cost (#$) for complete installation (less is BEST). Here the weight was "1" because the lowest score wins (like in golf).

- **Second Most Important:** Time to install (#Days) (less is BEST); you need this done quickly to minimize any disruption to operations. Here the weight was "2."

- **Least Important:** Number of positive customer referrals (more is BEST) because you needed the confidence that they could make this happen. Here the weight was "3."

At this point, you asked your team to either concur or non-concur with the work completed thus far. Non-concurring reasons were resolved within the team. After some open and candid discussion, all members concurred that they could follow, execute, and support the results thus far, so the process could move forward.

Step 4.2: Analyze the Advantages and Disadvantages:

Three days later, all 10-Vendors submitted their bids. Your team then confirmed the number of positive referrals. When all the results were in, you asked your team to identify the Advantages (benefits or upside) and Disadvantages (consequences or downside) for each Vendor compared to the *Evaluative Criteria* without comparing them.

Vendor A		
Criteria	**Advantages**	**Disadvantages**
Cost		
Time		
# Positive Referrals		
Screening		
Results: Did it pass or fail (reasons)?		

They did this for each Vendor, one at a time. After applying the *Evaluative Criteria* (5-Vendors submitted bids over $200,000 and were screened out from consideration as too expensive). Only these 5-Vendors remained, and here is the final data from their bids.

Raw Data Decision Matrix 1 (as of Feb 21, 20XX)					
Criterion	Vendors				
	A	B	C	D	E
Cost (K$)	150K	200K	160K	190K	170K
Time (Days)	45	38	40	42	48
# Pos. Referrals	12	21	4	17	11

At this point, you again asked your team to either concur or non-concur with the work completed thus far. Non-concurring reasons were resolved within the team. After some open and candid discussion, one member had a *Reason for Non-Support*. One member had a *valid reason for non-support*, and you decided to discuss it further. You displayed it up on the wall for all to see and began to conduct a *Brainstorming* Session.

Here, you asked for potential solutions from all members to address the *Reason for Non-Support*. After much discussion, adjustments were made, and all members finally "concurred" that they could follow, support, and execute the results thus far. So, the process was able to move forward. In your pursuit of the BEST Vendor, you continued to focus on your *Unresolved Issues List*.

Step 4.3: Compare Possible Solutions:

The next day, you continued by comparing all 5-Vendors together (against each other), as shown below.

Vendor	Advantages	Disadvantages
A	Least Cost	2d Highest Time to Install
B	Most # Referrals, Lowest Time Install	Highest Cost
C	2d Lowest Time to Install, 2d Lowest Cost	2d Lowest # Referrals
D	2d Highest # Referrals	2d Highest Cost
E	None	Most Time to Install

You also added the weighting to the Initial *Decision Matrix* to create your Weighted *Decision Matrix* 2, as shown below.

Weighted Decision Matrix 2 (as of Feb 21, 20XX)

Criterion	Weight	Vendors				
		A	B	C	D	E
Cost (K$)	1	150K	200K	160K	190K	170K
Time (Days)	2	45	38	40	42	48
# Pos. Referrals	3	12	21	4	17	11

In the Weighted *Decision Matrix* 2, each *Evaluative Criteria* was weighted. Since only 5 Vendors are remaining, you're ready to assign their Rank Order numbers using the Formula: The lowest number is the winner (like in a game of Golf).

Therefore, under Total $Cost, since Vendor A was the least expensive at $150 K, you placed a (1) in the cell with 150 K signifying that Vendor A was the least expensive. Since Vendor B was the most expensive, you placed a (5) in the cell with 200 K, and so forth, until all rank order numbers were in each box, as shown below. You did the same thing for each *Evaluative Criteria*.

Weighted Decision Matrix 2 (as of Feb 21, 20XX)

Criterion	Weight	Vendors				
		A	B	C	D	E
Cost ($K)	1	150K (1)	200K (5)	160K (2)	190K (4)	170K (3)
Time (#Days)	2	45 (4)	38 (1)	40 (2)	42 (3)	48 (5)
# Pos. Referrals	3	12 (3)	21 (1)	4 (5)	17 (2)	11 (4)

In the Weighted *Decision Matrix* 2, you removed all Total $Cost, #Days, and #Referrals from the matrix, leaving only the rank order numbers in parenthesis (....) that represented each Vendor ranked in each *Evaluative Criteria*, as shown below.

Final Decision Matrix 3 (as of Feb 21, 20XX)						
Criterion	Weight	Vendors				
		A	B	C	D	E
Cost (K$)	1	(1)	(5)	(2)	(4)	(3)
Time (Days)	2	(4)	(1)	(2)	(3)	(5)
# Pos. Referrals	3	(3)	(1)	(5)	(2)	(4)

Then, in the Final *Decision Matrix 3*, you simply multiplied the weighted value times its associated Rank Order number (the number in parenthesis (....)).

Next, you added the scores vertically in each column, as shown below.

Weighted Decision Matrix 3 (as of Feb 21, 20XX)						
Criterion	Wt.	Vendors				
		A	B	C	D	E
Cost ($K)	1	1 X (1) = 1	1 X (5) = 5	1 X (2) = 2	1 X (4) = 4	1 X (3) = 3
Time (#Days)	2	2 X (4) = 8	2 X (1) = 2	2 X (2) = 4	2 X (3) = 6	2 X (5) = 10
# Pos. Referrals	3	3 X (3) = 9	3 X (1) = 3	3 X (5) = 15	3 X (2) = 6	3 X (4) = 12
Total		18	10 Best	21	16	25

In summary, you and your team found that Vendor B had the lowest total score. However, *The Problem-Solving Process* doesn't make the final decision. The PSP only arrays the Vendors from BEST (lowest score) to Worst (highest score). So, you still need to decide.

Step 5:
Select the BEST
(Lowest Score Wins)

THE LOWEST SCORE = **VENDOR B**

You didn't have to choose the Vendor with the lowest score. And, if Vendor B backs out (or your boss reduces his funding), you can refer to your Final *Decision Matrix 3* and contact Vendor D because he was the 2d BEST (lowest) choice. So, the next day, you worked with your team to estimate the consequences and effects of choosing Vendor B, and here are your results.

Assess the Consequences and Effects:

The *Unintended Consequences* of hiring Vendor B are:

- Positive: This will increase our sales and enhance customer support
- Negative: This new system could crash – then what?

2d and 3d Order Effects of hiring Vendor B are:

- Team: We all need to get trained on this new system.
- Unit: This will affect other units we support due to new reporting procedures and formats.
- Organization: No adverse effects, only positive.

Before the final decision was made, you once again asked your team to concur or non-concur to the selection of Vendor B to do the work. Again, non-concurring reasons were resolved within the team. After some open and candid discussion, all members concurred to follow, execute, and support Vendor B being selected to upgrade the IT Infrastructure.

Now you have what you need to make a final decision. The next day you and your team prepared your *Plan of Action (POA)* for the installation in preparation for *Staffing* it through your company's Senior Management.

E
"DON'T FORGIT NOTHIN"

Have you ever created a plan but later found that you left things out? Effective people have checklists to remind them of all the things they need to consider. Here are some examples:

- **Communications:** Do you have direct communication with your Key Players via cell phone or 2-way radios with backup batteries and chargers? Does everyone have a list of each other's phone numbers? What if they're not near their cell phone when you call (or are on another call)?

- **Fun:** Laughter, humor, music, breaks, snacks, games, awards, recognition, surprises, and prizes.

- **Getting attendees involved:** How can you put attendees to work? Have them physically do simulations, problem-solving, breakout sessions, circuit training, seminars, workshops, round-robin stations, role-playing, practical exercises, competition, or small group discussions.

- **Headquarters:** Is there a known location at the event or activity, with a dedicated phone number that's open 24/7 that tracks attendance, safety, and first aid. Do they have a vehicle, driver, and map to the nearest hospital?

- **Life Support:** How will the participants be physically sustained (includes food, drink, snacks, ice, communications, lodging (if overnight), transportation, hygiene, toilets, electricity, cooking, refrigeration, liability insurance, sanitation (hand sanitizer, toilet paper), overhead shelter (if it rains), trash containers, and trash collection and removal). The longer the time and distance from home base, the more complicated the life support becomes.

- **Pre-work:** Do you want the participants to do something before the event and bring it with them? Do they need to review a read-ahead packet? If so, provide it in advance.

- **Program Support:** Audio and visual aids, handouts, loud-speaker, music, surveys, or backup generators?

- **Promotion:** How can you best advertise the event or activity that creates interest and anticipation? What's in it for them? What would make members want to attend? How will you communicate this to all invitees?

- **Quality Control (Assessment):** IPRs, AARs, meetings, deliverables, accountability, surveys, Contingency and Mitigation Plans, Project Updates, metrics, milestones, Timetables, and achieving consensus?

- **Rehearsals:** What do you need to see before you start? Do you need to practice, preview, or rehearse anything before the event/activity? Who is reviewing documents to see if they make sense and are correct?

- **Safety and Medical:** What if someone gets hurt? Do you need first aid kits, defibrillators, life jackets (if around water), and fire extinguishers? Are there any other hazards (like holes, cliffs, water, or any way anyone could get hurt)? How can you mitigate this risk? Do you need members trained in CPR and first aid? How about Bee stings (EpiPen® need a prescription), bug spray, location of the nearest hospital, vehicle designated to transport, maps to hospital, cell phones with 911 capabilities, and is there an ambulance needed on the site?

- **Schedule or Program:** Is there ample time built into the program for all to have fun and do something meaningful instead of just sitting there? How about a mixer (with name tags) so members can get to meet and know each other?

- **Search Plan:** What happens when someone is reported "missing," especially if away from the organization's property?

- **Security:** Are chaperones, guards, police, crowd and traffic control, or checkers needed? Cell phones (with chargers/extra batteries), cameras, and phone# available? Are metal detectors needed to check for weapons?

- **Site Transition:** Site problems also include the poor scheduling of other units before and after your scheduled time. The concern here is that the previous unit may not be cleared of the site before you try to set-up. And this includes your departure at the end of your project before the next unit attempts to move in. Additionally, many units try to pre-stage and move supplies and equipment the night before the project. Ensure you know who'll be there before you and who is coming in after you to ensure the handoff is smooth.

- **Small Children:** Children are a special challenge because they're so mobile and seem to find their way, unsupervised, into places where they could potentially get hurt. If there's water, you'll need life vests, lifeguards, and the like. If there's a fire or anything hot, or vehicle traffic, wells, or cliffs - get the idea?

- **Time:** What are the start and end times? What else is going on around the selected site during this time? What else is going on in the lives of those assigned to perform certain activities like graduations, summer vacations, or the Super Bowl? Hint? What happened last year at the same time and place? What's your *Contingency Plan*?

- **Other:** Parking, access for delivery vehicles, traffic flow, who tracks who's there and who's not? Do you have a backup location in case of bad weather? Did you *delegate all these tasks? Do you have consensus from all Key Players?

Note: You may not need all these reminders for your next project, but it's a nice checklist to add to your toolbox.

*To learn more about *Delegating,* available at **Amazon.com,** see page 5.

What are you forgetting to do?

Murphy's 5th Corollary.

Whatever you start to do, there will always be something you should have done first.

This page is intentionally left blank.

F
TAKE IMMEDIATE ACTION

When bad things happen, what do you usually do? Don't just sit there, do something! But what?

Immediate Action is a proactive eight-step process used to react to any bad situation that could cause a work stoppage, property damage, a security breach, or physical injury.

Let's drill down on the eight steps of the *Immediate Action* process.

Step 1. Assess the Situation.

Either be *on-the-scene* or in communication with someone on the ground. Assess the situation based on the facts.

Step 2. Notify Emergency Services and your boss.

If needed, call 911, and call your boss to tell him what you know.

Step 3. Consider your Options.

Look around. What's available for you to use? What should be done to stabilize the situation? What are your options? If time permits, collaborate with others.

Step 4. Select the Best Option.

Select the best option, and if time permits, achieve consensus with those around you.

Step 5. Create a Plan of Action.

Create a quick mental *Plan of Action*. What's the first step? What's the second, and so forth?

Step 6. Take Decisive Action.

Using what's available, *take-charge*, and give new instructions to others. Supervise their actions.

Step 7. Reassess the Situation.

What, if anything, has changed? Did the situation stabilize, or was the problem resolved? If Yes, move to Step 8. If NO, repeat this process.

Step 8. Call your boss.

Keep your boss informed. Explain what happened, what caused it, and what you recommend be done to ensure this never happens again.

Sounds pretty easy, right? Well, let's see how it's done in the real world.

True Story

At 9 AM, two days before his company's annual Team Building Session, Bob, the Project Manager, conducted his final site inspection of the resort and was astonished by what he saw. He tried to pull into the resort, but it was blocked by construction vehicles tearing up the parking lot. This was a disaster for Bob because he had 50 Senior Executives flying in from all over the country for this session. Fortunately, Bob knew how to take Immediate Action.

Step 1. Assess the Situation.

Bob didn't panic. He assessed the situation, took photos with his cell phone, spoke with the resort manager, and learned that a major water main had broken, which meant that the resort had no water. Bob also talked to the on-site construction manager and learned that the water main could not be repaired for another week.

Step 2. Call Emergency Services and your boss.

At 9:30 AM: Since there was no need to call 911, Bob called his boss and appraised him of the situation.

Step 3. Consider your options.

At 10 AM, Bob called a meeting of all Key Players at company headquarters to collaborate to find the best solution. Bob asked one Key Player to find another venue that could accommodate 50 people. By 11 AM, a new venue had been found, but it was 27 miles from the airport. One problem was solved, but it created another. How will all attendees get from the airport to the resort? Someone asked, can't they just catch a cab or just rent a car at the airport? For 50 people to catch a cab or rent a car would be way too expensive.

Step 4. Select the best option.

Then someone suggested that they rent a fleet of shuttle vehicles with drivers to transport all attendees from the airport to the resort and back. They all agreed that this was the best solution.

Step 5. Create a Plan of Action.

Together they created a Plan of Action to use shuttle vehicles to accomplish the objective.

Step 6. Take Decisive Action.

Bob issued new instructions to all Key Players and supervised their actions. He assigned one Key Player to contact all attendees to let them know what happened and look for company signs at the airport directing them to shuttle vehicles rather than taking a cab or renting a vehicle. Bob also asked a second Key Player to identify and contract a shuttle company to transport all attendees. Finally, he asked everyone to meet again at 5 PM to share the status of their new assignments.

Step 7. Reassess the Situation.

At 5 PM that afternoon, Bob met with all Key Players to ensure everything was ready to move forward with a fleet of shuttle vehicles.

Step 8. Report to your boss.

At 6 PM, Bob called his boss and informed him that the problem was resolved by selecting a new site and renting a fleet of shuttle vans to drive all attendees from the airport to the hotel and back. There was no reason to recommend what needed to be done to ensure this didn't happen again. The Team Building Session went on without any further problems and turned out to be a great success.

Bob looked defeat in the eye and refused to give up,

"Snatching Victory from the Jaws of Defeat."

And you can do the same!

This page is intentionally left blank.

G
USE CRITICAL REASONING
& CREATIVE THINKING

Someday you'll be writing to convince someone to make a decision. You'll be writing to convince your boss, or his boss, to spend the money needed to move your work forward.

Successful projects require that you communicate well in writing. As viewed by your subordinates, peers, and superiors, your reputation and credibility will depend on your writing and speaking skills, which flow from the quality of your thoughts.

We all think; it's in our nature to do so. Unfortunately, however, much of what we think about every day is flawed, which means our thoughts are biased, distorted, partial, uninformed, and prejudiced.

It's part of being human. Unfortunately, we all fall prey to errors in reasoning, human irrationality, and self-interest - caused by our emotions.

The quality of what you say and do every day depends on the quality of your thoughts. Flawed thinking will cost you, both in money and in the quality of your life.

Excellence in thought, on the other hand, requires a more disciplined and systematic approach.

So, what are you to do? How can you cope with the complexities and ever-changing nature of business? Fortunately, there are two powerful *awareness skills that can help you overcome your human flaws: Critical Reasoning and Creative thinking.

By using Creative Thinking

Creative Thinking is your ability to see new possibilities or different ways of doing things by finding new strategies, innovative techniques, or unusual solutions.

It asks you to identify those inhibitors that focus your thinking along predetermined paths, including your perceptions, culture, environment, emotions, and intellect.

Creative Thinking involves skills like brainstorming and originality, which promotes divergent thinking and stimulates curiosity.

It's used to solve problems, deal with crises, improve products and processes, and deal with situations where new solutions are needed.

By using Critical Reasoning

Critical reasoning is your ability to logically examine your thoughts, choices, decisions, and recommendations for truth and validity before they're made.

Critical reasoning is a self-disciplined skill that attempts to reason more logically by asking better questions, considering alternatives, avoiding falling for the simple solution, and recognizing the consequence and effects your actions have on others.

And it helps identify the best solution to problems with maximum buy-in, which ultimately saves time, money, and stress. This skill includes researching, statistical analysis, classifying, recognizing patterns, forecasting, and making calculations.

These skills help you evaluate your thinking for relevance, consistency, accuracy, fairness, and completeness. And when you apply these skills to your writing process, you'll enhance your ability to communicate.

Remember, to become more effective; you'll need to be thinking one or two steps ahead of your boss; anticipate opportunities, see around corners and catch mistakes before they become problems, and smell out problems before they become a crisis.

H
ASSESS YOUR ACCOUNTABILITY

Do you know what to do when your boss finds something wrong with your work?

Accountability is the acceptance of responsibility for your actions and in-actions and the obligation to report, explain, and be answerable for any adverse consequences.

Accountability is often confused with responsibility. They're related but different. *Accountability* is normally not a problem - until something goes wrong.

For example, if something goes wrong within your area of responsibility, you'll get the chance to explain what happened to your boss, and maybe his boss. Sometimes, depending on the severity of the problem, your boss won't be happy with you and may treat you badly.

Most people don't understand that, yes, responsibility and *accountability* go together; they're part of the same iceberg.

However, you can't see the *accountability* part of the iceberg because it lies hidden beneath the surface until something goes wrong.

What should you do when things go wrong?

> When things go wrong for which you're responsible, your boss's job is to ask you for an explanation.

What your boss doesn't need is for you to complain, blame others, make excuses, or hide the truth.

And yes, the mistake may have been made by one of your team members - not you. But your boss doesn't care. He just wants it fixed.

Here's what your boss expects you to do:

Step 1. Step up and accept the blame!

Step 2. Investigate - what happened and what caused it to happen?

Step 3. Report the facts and recommend how it should be fixed.

Step 4. Fix it and fix it for good!

Step 5. When fixed, report the fix to your boss.

Step 6. Make sure it never happens again.

Accountability is something every boss expects from you but won't tell you until it's too late. But, unfortunately, this quality isn't something you were born with. And the only time you get to demonstrate your accountability is when things go wrong.

This also includes the actions, in-actions, and adverse consequences of those members within your charge. You're accountable to your boss for everything that happens or fails to happen within your area of responsibility.

However, *accountability* can't exist unless you know all the things for which you're responsible. For example, you can't be held *accountable* for your company's finances if your duties and responsibilities are to service rental cars.

Establish the reputation of being a good problem solver as well as a good problem finder. Your job is to help your boss find and eliminate all the obstacles that could slow or stop the achievement of his goals.

Remember, mistakes, errors, and defects are not a problem if they're caught and fixed before getting in front of your boss or the customer.

Self-Test
Are you Accountable?

Here are the most important questions to answer to assess your *accountability*.

1. *Do you do the right thing?*

At an early age, I learned these simple lessons about accountability:

- If you lose, damage, or break something that doesn't belong to you, you need to fix it or buy it.
- If you borrow something, you need to return it in the same or better condition than you found it.
- If you back into and damage someone's car, and they're not around, you need to leave a note on their windshield with your name and phone number to help repair the damage.
- If you were mean or disrespectful to someone, you need to apologize.

2. *Are you self-correcting?*

A self-correcting person is someone capable of correcting himself without external help.

Part of being *accountable* is being *self-correcting*, especially when starting a new position, even if it's within the same company. Starting anything new is all about learning what you need to know as soon as possible. I'm always amazed by those who never take notes. Why do so few people take notes anymore (with your cell phone or Rocket Book)?

"A short pencil is a long memory." – Unknown.

When you have a question, write it down. Many times, the person with the correct answer won't be immediately available. If you find a term you don't understand, write it down. Later, find out what the term means. Keep a list of all your questions and terms you don't understand. This list will help later when you sponsor a new member into your team. *Self-correcting* people take notes (they don't trust their memory), write down their questions and the answers, and are not afraid to ask questions and proactively seek answers.

3. Do you live your life with no excuses?

People make excuses because it has worked for them in the past. It avoids accepting *accountability*. They're testing your limits to see how much they can get away with, and they fear the consequences of their actions or inactions.

What's the difference between a reason and an excuse?

Here's a simple rule:

Reasons are believable, understandable, and forgivable.

Excuses aren't.

- **Denial:** Refusing to admit or acknowledge that their behavior is a problem. (Example: "I can stop swearing any time I want. My language isn't that bad.")
- **Isolation:** Removing themselves from the team area to maintain their behavior. (Example: "If I had my own office, this wouldn't be a problem.")
- **Rationalization:** Giving reasons to explain their behavior. (Example: "I screamed at him because he doesn't like me.")
- **Blaming (or Transferal):** Transferring *accountability* for their behavior to others. (Example: "I wouldn't be late all the time if my teammates treated me right.")
- **Projection:** Rejecting their feelings by ascribing them to another (Example: "Why is that stupid idiot so hostile?")
- **Minimizing or Trivialize:** Refusing to admit the effect of their behavior. (Example: "I only told one bad joke. It's not a big deal.")

They close their eyes to the destructive consequences of their unacceptable behavior, or they explain their actions in a way that saves them from having to feel. Either way, it's wrong and must be dealt with immediately.

4. Do you do your best work every day?

Here's a great story about doing your best work.

> *It's rumored that when Dr. **Henry Kissinger** was Secretary of State in the administrations of **Presidents Nixon and Ford**, he asked for a security assessment to be made of a foreign country. The first day, when a subordinate delivered the report, Secretary Kissinger asked, "Is this your best work?"*
>
> *The subordinate thought for a second and walked out of the office. The second day, the subordinate returned with the report, and Kissinger asked the same question. The subordinate again thought for a moment and walked back out of the office.*
>
> *On the third day, the subordinate returned, and Kissinger asked for the third time, "Is this your best work?" This time the subordinate said, "Yes." Kissinger then responded, "Good, now I'll read it."*

I share this story to highlight that there are no shortcuts to success. Your success will always be linked to *"doing your best work."* Do you do your best work every day? Would your boss agree?

5. Are you proactive?

Another thing that contributes to your effectiveness and success at work is your ability to be proactive.

A proactive person identifies and prevents potential problems by causing things to happen rather than reacting to them after they happen.

Proactive people:

- Identify potential pre-problems before they become a problem and problems before they become a crisis.

- Anticipate their boss's and customer's needs and expectations.

- Use Preventive Actions to identify and resolve all Pre-Problems.

- Take-charge and produce order in the midst of chaos.

- Use collaborative problem solving to build consensus (Chapter 24) and resolve Unresolved Issues (Chapter 32)

- Take Immediate Action (Appendix F) and don't wait to be told what to do.
- Anticipate Unintended Consequences and 2d and 3d Order Effects (Chapter 33)
- Manage risk (Chapters 26-28) and make things happen the right way the first time.

6. Do you make recommendations to your boss to make things better?

Your job is to help your boss achieve his goals. What do you do when you find a problem or an improvement that could make things better? Do you create a *Decision Paper* or a *Business Case* (Appendix E) to make it happen?

I've often written Decision Papers through my boss to his boss because my boss didn't have the funding to make it happen. As shown below, the Decision Paper was addressed "To," my boss's boss, "Thru," my boss.

To: My boss's boss.

Thru: My boss.

From: Me

My boss would then initial and write "Approved" next to the "Thru" line above and send it to his boss for final approval. This process helped my boss move the work forward.

If you cannot answer these questions with a strong YES, you need to reassess your *accountability*. Effective people take this assessment annually and fix what needs to be fixed.

ACKNOWLEDGMENTS

"Many people will walk in and out of your life, but only true friends will leave footprints in your heart."
- Eleanor Roosevelt

I'd like to recognize those with whom I've had the pleasure of serving, whose effectiveness and character I vividly recall, many of whom are not here today to tell their story.

For my military career, I thank Betty McIntee, Edward J. Murphy (my Dad), Dale R. Nelson, Geoffrey "Jeff" Prosch, Craig "Randy" Rutler, Dave Wagner, John Andrews, John "The Bear" Warren, John "Jack" Costello, Dan Labin, and Ron Nicholl for their example of effectiveness.

For my coaching career, I thank Tony Robbins, Bernard Haldane, Jack Bissell, Len Drew, Wayne McCullum, Bob Schrier, John Hurtig, and Bob Gerberg for their mentoring and coaching.

Special thanks to my long-time mentor and friend, Joyce Kuntz, who encouraged me to write this book. After leaving the US Military, Joyce was my first and best boss when I joined her consulting firm in Seattle years ago. Unfortunately, Joyce is gone now, but her legacy lives on in this book.

"I must be able to say with sincerity that to see things differently is a strength, not a weakness, in my relationship with others."
- Joyce Kuntz

I thank Joyce's husband, Ed Kuntz, who turned out to be the man who brought me to Seattle from Kansas City to start my incredible second career as an Executive Coach.

And finally, I thank my soulmate and wife, **Diana**, for her love, encouragement, and understanding throughout this process.

When I count my blessings, I always count her twice.

This page is intentionally left blank.

ABOUT THE AUTHOR

"I expect to pass through this world but once; any good thing therefore that I can do, or any kindness that I can show to any fellow creature, let me do it now; let me not defer or neglect it, for I shall not pass this way again."
- Stephan Grelle

Ed Murphy considers himself lucky. From age 7, he knew what he wanted to be when he grew up. He wanted to be a Soldier. So, four days after graduating from High School, he joined the US Army and found himself in Basic Training and Advanced Infantry Training at Fort Dix, New Jersey.

A year later, Ed became a Cadet at the United States Military Academy at West Point. In 1970, he graduated as a 2d Lieutenant headed to Airborne and Ranger School, then off to Viet Nam for a year.

In 1978, Ed returned to West Point to teach Military Science and earned an MS from LIU in night school. During his tenure as a Battalion Commander in West Germany, his greatest achievement was helping 1400 soldiers begin a college education. He wanted to give his soldiers something of real value - something that no one could ever take away. After 23 years as a US Army Officer, he retired in 1993.

For his second career, with a little help from *Tony Robbins*, he became an Executive Coach. Then, for the next 21 years, he worked for four of the largest career development and outplacement companies in America, from Seattle, San Diego, Kansas City, and Phoenix.

In 2012, Ed retired a second time and decided to document everything he learned from those he most admired during his 50+ years in the US Military as an Army Officer and Corporate America as an Executive Coach.

In 2014, he began writing books for Amazon and Kindle dedicated to providing the best-in-class wisdom, knowledge, and advice to help others maximize their true career potential by becoming more effective and successful at work and in life.

Today, Ed considers himself blessed to live in Phoenix, AZ. He enjoys writing, eating sushi, genealogy, and watching movies with family, friends, and his best friend and wife, **Diana**.

This page is intentionally left blank.

CONCLUSION

Congratulations!

And thank you for joining us on this *Journey of Discovery*.

As promised, you now have a *Training Guide* to add to your professional library - the one I never had.

Every effective boss needs effective followers who can consistently produce excellent results and add value to those who helped produce those results.

You now have the most actionable *Training Skills* you were never taught in school or college to support you throughout your career.

Now it's your turn to apply and share this new knowledge to add greater value to your boss and all those with whom you serve.

These are the essential *Best Practices* I've learned over the past 50 years to help you become far more effective and successful than you were yesterday.

As always, I wish you great success.

Never STOP Learning!

Ed

Founder of *The Effectiveness Institute*
email: ed.murphy77@gmail.com

PS: Also, if you feel this information could help someone else, please let them know. If it turns out to make a difference in their life, they'll be forever grateful to you, as will I.

Stop wishing you were better and do something about it today.

www.ingramcontent.com/pod-product-compliance
Lightning Source LLC
Chambersburg PA
CBHW071431180526
45170CB00001B/304